Recreational Wonders

Navigating National Parks in Your Home on Wheels

Lucas Adams

Table of Contents

INTRODUCTION **6**

CHAPTER I: The RV Lifestyle **7**

Understanding the appeal of RV living 7

Types of RVs and their features 9

Budgeting for RV travel.................................... 11

Essential equipment and accessories 13

CHAPTER II: Planning Your RV Adventure **17**

Choosing the right national parks 17

Seasonal considerations 20

Reservations and permits 22

Route planning and itineraries 24

CHAPTER III: Hitting the Road **28**

Preparing your RV for departure 28

Safety tips for RV travel 30

Driving and navigation tips 33

Staying connected on the road 36

CHAPTER IV: National Park Essentials **40**

Introduction to the National Park Service (NPS) 40

Park pass options 43

Park rules and regulations 46

Leave No Trace principles 48

CHAPTER V: Making the Most of Your Park Visits........... 51

Selecting the best campgrounds 51

Exploring Park visitor centers 54

Participating in ranger-led programs 56

Choosing and planning hikes 59

CHAPTER VI: RV Camping in National Parks 63

Campground options within parks 63

Reservations vs. first-come, first-served 65

RV hookups and amenities 67

Boondocking and dry camping 70

CHAPTER VII: Outdoor Activities 74

Hiking and backpacking 74

Wildlife watching 76

Photography opportunities 79

Water-based activities 81

CHAPTER VIII: Navigating the Parks Responsibly 85

Leave No Trace principles for RVers 85

Wildlife safety 87

Managing waste and environmental impact 90

Fire safety in the great outdoors 92

CHAPTER IX: Exploring Nearby Attractions 96

Off-the-beaten-path destinations 96

Local culture and history 99

Dining and shopping recommendations 102

Side trips and day excursions 105

CHAPTER X: Staying Healthy and Safe 108

Health and medical considerations 108

Emergency preparedness 110

Personal safety on the road.. 112

Coping with unexpected challenges 114

CHAPTER XI: Wrapping Up Your Adventure 117

Packing up and preparing to leave 117

Reflections on your RV journey 119

Documenting your travels 121

Planning for future adventures 123

CONCLUSION 126

INTRODUCTION

Imagine being surrounded by towering forests, majestic mountains, or the serene beauty of a pristine lake when you wake up to the peaceful sounds of birdsong. The comfort of your home never changes, even though the world outside your window does. This is the charm of camping in the breathtaking national parks of America.

The book "Recreational Wonders: Navigating National Parks in Your Home on Wheels" is your ticket to an unparalleled adventure. From the comfortable confines of your home on wheels, we will travel through some of America's most famous and varied natural landscapes in the following pages.

For many years, the RV lifestyle has captivated the interest of travelers, adventurers, and outdoors lovers. It provides the ideal balance of comfort, freedom, and flexibility, allowing you to bring home comforts and take in the breathtaking scenery of national parks. This book is your tour guide, friend, and itinerary as you explore the recreational wonders and undiscovered gems waiting for you.

This book will assist you in organizing your next exciting trip, regardless of your level of experience traveling in an RV. "Recreational Wonders" is your all-inclusive guide to turning your ideal RV trip into a reality, from picking the perfect RV and negotiating the complexities of national park regulations to finding hidden hiking trails and taking breathtaking pictures with your camera.

So buckle up, pack up your belongings, and get ready to explore the vast American outdoors from the comfort of your mobile home. This is where the adventure starts.

CHAPTER I

The RV Lifestyle

Understanding the appeal of RV living

Living in a recreational vehicle (RV), also known as the "RV lifestyle," has captivated the interest and wanderlust of individuals from diverse backgrounds. It's a lifestyle that challenges accepted conventions, enabling people and families to embrace a mobile and adventurous existence and free themselves from the constraints of a stationary one. There are several aspects to RV living's appeal, which appeal to various individuals.

The quest for freedom lies at the core of the RV lifestyle.

For many RV enthusiasts, the ability to travel, explore, and see new places at their own pace is a powerful allure. The thought of waking up one morning amid the majesty of the Rocky Mountains and the next by a calm coastal inlet is an alluring promise in a world where routines and schedules frequently control our lives. With their unique combination of independence and mobility, recreational vehicles (RVs) allow people to choose their own path and make impulsive decisions about where to go and when. Additionally, RV living offers an unmatched connection to the great outdoors. Because this lifestyle puts them in the middle of some of the most breathtaking landscapes the world provides, nature lovers are drawn to it. RV living places you right in the middle of nature's beauties, whether camping beneath towering redwoods, parking next to a spotless alpine lake, or waking up to waves crashing on a sandy beach. It's a call to fully embrace the natural beauty and tranquility of the surroundings, cultivating a profound understanding of the variety of ecosystems worldwide.

Those looking for a smaller, more straightforward lifestyle also find appeal in the RV lifestyle. Moving down to a tiny, mobile home is becoming increasingly alluring in a world where materialism and consumerism are prevalent. Living in an RV encourages people to assess their belongings and determine what is most important. This way of living promotes minimalism and a sense of freedom from the excess and clutter that frequently drags people down. Living in an RV makes one realize that experiences, not material belongings, are what truly bring happiness.

An additional important component of the RV lifestyle is social interaction. While traveling, RVers frequently create tight-knit groups where they exchange stories, advice, and friendship. RV parks and campgrounds develop into hubs of social interaction where people from all walks of life gather to celebrate their mutual love of exploration and adventure. These connections transcend age, occupation, and cultural differences, making RV living an inclusive and welcoming community.

Living in an RV appeals to some people financially. Living in an RV may be less expensive than living in a traditional home. Buying an RV can result in long-term financial savings despite the high initial cost. Money for experiences and travel can be made available by lowering maintenance expenses, property taxes, and utility bills. RVers can also work remotely, allowing them to make a living while taking advantage of the freedom of traveling.

Moreover, living in an RV offers a unique personal development and self-discovery opportunity. It tests people's ability to accept change, adapt to new surroundings, and solve problems quickly. It promotes personal growth and a stronger sense of self-reliance by encouraging a resilient and flexible mindset.

In conclusion, RV living has many different and intensely personal aspects. People who value independence, a connection to nature, simplicity, social interaction, financial flexibility, and personal development will find resonance in this way of living. Many see it as a conscious decision to leave the constraints of a traditional life behind and embark on an adventure-filled journey involving travel, discovery, and the pursuit of happiness. Living in an RV offers the opportunity to experience life to the fullest and is more than just a means of transportation.

Types of RVs and their features

Recreational vehicles (RVs) are made to accommodate a wide range of needs, tastes, and lifestyles. They are available in a variety of sizes and shapes. The world of recreational vehicles (RVs) provides options for single travelers and large families looking for adventure on the road, ranging from small camper vans to roomy motorhomes. When choosing an RV that best fits your needs and travel style, it's essential to understand the different kinds of RVs and their distinctive features.

The camper van is among the RV world's most compact options. These cars are basically vans that have been customized to include living, sleeping, and kitchen spaces. Couples or lone travelers seeking portability and ease of use should consider camper vans. They're great for quick road trips or weekend getaways because they're simple to drive and frequently fit into regular parking spaces. Despite their reduced size, modern camper vans provide innovative space-saving features like fold-down beds, small kitchens, and effective storage.

RV enthusiasts often opt for the travel trailer due to its increased size and amenities. Several different types of trailers are available for these, such as the standard travel trailer, fifth-wheel trailer, and toy hauler. The ability to be towed by a different vehicle—usually a truck or SUV—is the primary characteristic of travel trailers. This eliminates the need for RVers to drive their accommodations everywhere, allowing them to set up camp and explore the neighborhood. Travel trailers are ideal for families, couples, and even larger groups because they come in various sizes and floor plans. They frequently have cozy sleeping quarters, kitchens, and bathrooms.

Motorhomes are the preferred option for people looking for a self-contained mobile home. RVs with built-in engines, known as motorhomes, do not require an additional towing car. Class A, Class B, and Class C are their three main classes. Class A models resemble tour buses, the largest and most expensive motorhomes. They have roomy interiors with multiple bedrooms, full-sized kitchens, and lots of storage. Camper vans, sometimes called class B motorhomes, are smaller but still provide the convenience of a single unit. Generally speaking, they are more maneuverable than Class A motorhomes. Class C motorhomes compromise space and mobility, making them a good option. They can easily fit families and frequently have a unique sleeping area over the cab.

The truck camper is a less famous but fascinating option in the world of RVs. These small units make for a convenient and portable living space that can be placed on the bed of a pickup truck. Truck campers are perfect for off-road adventures and allow for quick setup at remote locations. Even though they might not have all the amenities of larger RVs, they still provide a distinctive and daring way to experience nature.

Teardrop trailers have become increasingly popular in recent years among people looking for a lightweight and compact RV alternative. These trailers are recognizable by their teardrop shape and aerodynamic design. Usually intended for two people, teardrop trailers have a cozy sleeping area and a small kitchenette at the back. They provide a comfortable and effective camping experience and are simple to tow.

Lastly, toy haulers are a fun option for people who enjoy outdoor toys and adventure sports. With the garage space built into the back of these RVs, you can transport kayaks, ATVs, motorcycles, and other equipment. For adventure seekers who wish to mix their passion of the great outdoors with RV living, toy haulers are ideal. The garage area can also be converted into additional sleeping or living space when not hauling equipment.

In conclusion, the world of RVs offers various options to suit various preferences and travel styles. There is an RV type to suit your needs, whether you value luxury, off-road capability, maneuverability, or the capacity to tow outdoor toys. When choosing an RV, it's essential to know the features and advantages of each kind because these will affect how comfortable and enjoyable your travels will be. Regardless of your preference, living in an RV offers you flexibility, adventure, and the chance to make lifelong travel memories.

Budgeting for RV travel

Many people have a dream of traveling in an RV because it gives them the freedom to discover new locations and make lifelong memories while driving. Like all forms of travel, though, there are expenses involved that must be properly managed. Planning your budget is essential to ensuring you can enjoy your adventure without worrying about running out of money while traveling in an RV.

The initial investment in the RV itself is one of the first things to consider when creating a budget for RV travel. Buying an RV can come at a considerable price difference depending on the kind, size, and condition of the vehicle. New RVs often come with a higher price tag, while used ones may offer cost savings. It's critical to ascertain your spending limit and consider all your options. Additionally, as this will affect your ongoing budget, consider whether you'll pay for the RV outright or through a loan.

After the initial purchase cost, fuel, park fees, and maintenance are additional expenses associated with RV travel. Your budget may include a sizable portion for fuel, particularly if you intend to travel large distances. It's critical to calculate your fuel costs based on the fuel efficiency of the RV and your planned route. RVs can occasionally need servicing and repairs, so it's a good idea to budget for unforeseen costs. Having a contingency fund can also give you peace of mind.

Another critical component of planning a budget for RV travel is campground fees. Campgrounds come in various configurations and price points, ranging from basic, rustic sites with few amenities to fully equipped, resort-style campgrounds with lots of amenities. Your budget will be significantly impacted by the campgrounds you choose. Plan ahead and do your homework to ensure you are aware of the prices and facilities that each campground has to offer. To cut costs at campgrounds, some travelers also consider alternatives like boondocking, which is free camping on public land.

Grocery and food costs should be included in your trip budget. Being able to cook for yourself while traveling in an RV can result in financial savings over eating out. Plan your groceries and meals carefully, and consider cooking in your RV a fun adventure. While traveling to new places, use the local farmers' markets and grocery stores to fill up on fresh produce.

Your budget should account for activities and entertainment. While certain activities might be inexpensive or free, others, like guided tours or attraction admission fees, can get expensive. Decide which tasks are most important to you, then set aside money for them. Consider the recreational activities you'll engage in while traveling, like hiking, fishing, or photography, and set aside money for supplies or gear.

You should budget for the non-negotiable expense of RV insurance. The type of RV you drive, your driving history, and the coverage options you choose can all affect the insurance price. Ensure you and your investment are sufficiently covered by insurance for your RV in case of mishaps or unanticipated circumstances.

While traveling, one should also think about purchasing health insurance. Anywhere can experience a medical emergency, so having sufficient health insurance is crucial for mental stability. Some RVers select health insurance plans with nationwide coverage, which enables them to get medical care wherever they are.

Finally, allocate funds for unforeseen circumstances and other non-essential costs. You can travel in an RV with less stress if you have savings for unexpected expenses. Costs for things like laundry, internet access, toiletries, and any unplanned emergencies can be included in this.

In conclusion, budgeting for RV travel is vital to ensuring a successful and enjoyable journey. The dream of traveling in an RV can come true with careful planning and budgeting, even though the initial cost and continuing expenses may seem overwhelming. Establishing and adhering to a clear budget and being realistic about your financial situation is critical. Being proactive and organized will allow you to travel in your RV confidently, knowing that all the expenses have been covered. You can then concentrate on the excitement of seeing new places and making priceless memories while traveling.

Essential equipment and accessories

Starting an RV adventure is a thrilling way to explore and travel the world. Having the appropriate tools and accessories can make all the difference in guaranteeing a cozy, risk-free, and joyful travel experience with RVs, regardless of experience level. This section examines the essential gear and accessories you should consider when getting ready for your RV travel adventure, from creature comforts to practical necessities.

When traveling in an RV, safety should come first and foremost. Carbon monoxide, smoke, and fire extinguishers are examples of basic safety equipment. In an emergency, these gadgets can literally save lives by offering vital tools and early warnings of potential risks. Make sure these safety devices are in working order by giving them regular maintenance and inspections.

An extensive first-aid kit is another essential safety factor. Accidents and minor injuries can happen anywhere, so keeping a fully stocked first-aid kit nearby can help when needed. Make sure your kit has all the necessities, such as bandages, antiseptic wipes, painkillers, and any personal medications you or your traveling companions might need.

An excellent RV leveling system is essential for comfort and convenience. RV leveling is crucial for safe sleeping conditions, efficient appliance operation, and preventing possible damage to your vehicle. Depending on the size and style of your RV, leveling blocks, leveling jacks, or electronic leveling systems are common choices.
Having a kitchen when traveling in an RV is a great benefit. Invest in an RV kitchen that is well-equipped to maximize the efficiency and enjoyment of this experience. This includes necessary appliances such as a refrigerator, microwave, stove, and oven. Before you hit the road, ensure these appliances are operating well. To prepare and enjoy meals on the go, make sure your kitchen is stocked with cookware, utensils, dishes, and cutlery.

Another essential component of RV travel is water. Connecting to campground water sources requires a freshwater hose and a water pressure regulator. An RV sewer hose support and a sewer hose are needed for effective waste disposal. Also, to be flexible with various campsite configurations, consider packing extra freshwater and wastewater hoses.

A solar power system or generator can be extremely helpful in scenarios where electrical hookups are limited or for off-grid camping. These power sources give your RV the electricity it needs to run appliances, charge electronics, and keep a cozy living space. Determine how much power you need, then select a solar or generator system that works for you.

Think about investing in climate control equipment to keep your home at a comfortable temperature. Although most RVs have built-in heating and cooling systems, space heaters and portable fans can be used to help control the temperature in particular areas. Thermal curtains or window coverings can also help keep your RV warm in the winter and cool in the summer.

The RV experience includes a lot of outdoor living, and the correct accessories can make you appreciate the outdoors even more. Awnings or shade structures can create an outdoor living area while shielding people from the sun. A foldable table and chairs come in handy for meals, unwinding, and mingling with other campers.

A TV antenna system or satellite can offer news, entertainment, and communication in terms of connectivity and entertainment. For internet access in remote areas, a lot of RVers also depend on satellite internet or mobile hotspot devices. Choose the right equipment by taking into account your communication and entertainment needs.

Always have cleaning supplies on hand, including vacuum cleaners, dustpans, mops, and brooms, to maintain a sanitary living area. RV-specific cleaning supplies can assist you in keeping your car's exterior and interior in good condition. Waste disposal accessories like disposable gloves and waste tank treatments are necessary to handle sewage and gray water properly.

Finally, maximizing the space in your RV requires a well-organized and effective storage system. Organizers, racks, and storage bins can help you make the most of your storage space and protect your possessions when you're traveling. To make it simple to identify the contents of each container, use clear containers.

In conclusion, having the proper tools and accessories for your RV is crucial to a successful and pleasurable road trip. The appropriate equipment can improve your RV travel experience, regardless of your comfort, safety, convenience, or entertainment priorities. Ensure your RV trip is full of comfort, fun, and treasured memories by carefully evaluating your needs, keeping your equipment in good working order, and investing in high-quality accessories.

CHAPTER II

Planning Your RV Adventure

Choosing the right national parks

Embarking on an RV travel adventure through America's national parks is a dream come true for many nature enthusiasts and adventure seekers. The United States boasts a vast and diverse array of national parks, each with unique landscapes, ecosystems, and recreational opportunities. Choosing the right national parks for your RV journey is a crucial decision that can significantly impact your overall experience. This section will explore key factors to consider when selecting national parks for RV travel and highlight some of the top parks that offer an unforgettable RV adventure.

When choosing national parks for RV travel, one of the first considerations is your personal interests and preferences. Are you drawn to the rugged beauty of the Rocky Mountains, the captivating deserts of the Southwest, or the pristine shorelines of coastal parks? Do you prefer hiking, viewing wildlife, photography, or simply relaxing outdoors? Identifying your interests and travel goals will help you narrow down your options and create a tailored itinerary.

Accessibility and location are also vital factors to take into account. Consider the geographic region you'd like to explore and the distance you're willing to travel to reach your chosen parks. Proximity to major cities, highways, and airports may influence your decision, especially if you plan to incorporate other attractions or side trips into your RV journey.

RV-friendly campgrounds and facilities are essential for a comfortable and hassle-free experience. Check if the national parks on your list offer RV campgrounds with suitable amenities such as electric hookups, water, sewage disposal, and spacious sites that can accommodate your RV size. Availability and reservation policies should also be considered, as some popular parks may have limited RV sites, requiring advanced booking.

The time of year you plan to travel can significantly impact your national park choices. Some parks are best enjoyed during specific seasons. For instance, parks like Joshua Tree or Zion in the Southwest are ideal for winter travel to escape the cold, while parks in the northern states are more pleasant in the summer months. Additionally, some parks may have seasonal road closures or limited accessibility during the winter, so it's essential to plan your visit accordingly.

Another factor to consider is the level of RV experience and comfort you desire. Some national parks offer a more rustic and off-grid camping experience, which can be rewarding for experienced RVers seeking solitude and adventure. Others, like Grand Canyon National Park or Yellowstone National Park, provide a range of amenities and services, making them suitable for RVers who prefer a more comfortable and well-equipped experience. Environmental considerations are vital when choosing national parks for RV travel. The Leave No Trace principles emphasize responsible outdoor ethics and should guide your decision-making. Some parks may have specific regulations and restrictions regarding RV camping, waste disposal, and wilderness protection. Research and adhere to these guidelines to minimize your impact on the environment and preserve the beauty of these natural treasures for future generations.

To help you get started on your RV adventure, here are a few national parks known for their RV-friendly facilities and stunning landscapes:

1. Yellowstone National Park: Located in Wyoming, Montana, and Idaho, Yellowstone is known for its geothermal wonders, including geysers and hot springs. The park offers RV campgrounds with various amenities and access to iconic attractions like Old Faithful.

2. Grand Teton National Park: Adjacent to Yellowstone, Grand Teton National Park is renowned for its towering peaks, pristine lakes, and abundant wildlife. RV campgrounds within the park provide excellent access to hiking and photography opportunities.

3. Acadia National Park: Located on the coast of Maine, Acadia offers a unique blend of rugged shoreline, lush forests, and mountainous terrain. RVers can enjoy scenic drives, hiking trails, and ocean views from within the park.

4. Zion National Park: In southwestern Utah, Zion is famous for its towering red rock formations and stunning canyons. The Watchman Campground offers RV sites, and the park provides shuttle services to explore its wonders.

5. Arches National Park: Also in Utah, Arches is home to over 2,000 natural sandstone arches. The park's Devils Garden Campground accommodates RVs and provides access to hiking trails that lead to these geological marvels.

6. Everglades National Park: Located in Florida, the Everglades is a unique wetland ecosystem teeming with wildlife. RV campgrounds are available, allowing you to explore the park's waterways and abundant birdlife.

7. Great Smoky Mountains National Park: Straddling the border between North Carolina and Tennessee, this park offers lush forests, cascading waterfalls, and diverse

wildlife. RV campgrounds are available, and the park is particularly beautiful in the fall.

In conclusion, choosing the suitable national parks for RV travel is a highly personal decision influenced by your interests, location preferences, RV experience level, and environmental responsibility. Careful research and planning will ensure you make the most of your RV adventure while experiencing the natural beauty and wonders of America's national parks. Whether you seek dramatic landscapes, outdoor adventures, or peaceful solitude, there's a national park waiting to fulfill your RV travel dreams.

Seasonal considerations

Embarking on an RV travel adventure can be a thrilling experience at any time of the year, but the season in which you choose to hit the road can significantly impact your journey. Each season offers its unique charms, challenges, and opportunities for RVers. Understanding the seasonal considerations for RV travel is crucial for planning a safe, enjoyable, and memorable trip.

Spring is a rejuvenating time for RV travel. As the weather warms, and the landscape awakens from its winter slumber, RVers can enjoy the beauty of blossoming flowers, budding trees, and mild temperatures. Many national parks and campgrounds come alive in spring, offering a quieter and more peaceful experience than the peak summer season. Spring is an excellent time for hiking, birdwatching, and enjoying the outdoors without the crowds. However, it's essential to be aware of unpredictable weather, as spring can bring rain showers and occasional late-season snow in some regions. It's also a prime time for allergies due to the abundance of pollen in the air.

Summer is the peak season for RV travel, with families and travelers flocking to national parks and campgrounds nationwide. The long days and warm weather make it an ideal time for outdoor adventures, swimming, and exploring. RVers can use extended daylight hours for hiking, fishing, and wildlife viewing. However, with the popularity of summer travel comes crowded campgrounds and popular destinations. Reservations for RV sites and activities are often essential, and flexibility may be limited. Additionally, be prepared for higher temperatures, especially in southern regions, and take precautions to stay cool and hydrated.

Autumn is a favored season for RV travel, particularly among those who relish the beauty of changing foliage. As leaves transform into vibrant shades of red, orange, and gold, RVers can witness breathtaking landscapes in national parks like the Great Smoky Mountains, Acadia, and Shenandoah. Cooler temperatures make outdoor activities more comfortable, and the absence of summer crowds means more peaceful and enjoyable experiences. Fall also brings harvest festivals, pumpkin patches, and apple picking opportunities along the way. However, planning ahead is important, as popular campgrounds and leaf-peeping destinations can fill up quickly. Be prepared for variable weather conditions as well, as autumn can bring chilly nights and unexpected rain.

Winter RV travel is for the adventurous souls who seek solitude and the magic of a winter wonderland. While many RVers choose to store their vehicles during the colder months, others embrace the snow-covered landscapes of national parks like Yellowstone and Glacier. Winter camping requires careful planning, focusing on cold-weather gear, insulation, and heating systems. It's also essential to check for seasonal road closures and campground availability, as many facilities may be limited or closed during the off-season. Winter RV travel can be rewarding for those who enjoy cross-country skiing, snowshoeing, and cozy evenings by the campfire, but it's not for the faint of heart.

In conclusion, the season in which you choose to embark on your RV travel adventure can significantly impact your experience. Each season offers its unique advantages and considerations, allowing RVers to tailor their trips to their preferences and interests. Whether you're seeking the vibrant blooms of spring, the excitement of a summer road trip, the picturesque foliage of autumn, or the tranquility of a winter escape, careful planning and preparation will ensure your RV journey is safe, enjoyable, and filled with unforgettable memories. Seasons change, but the joy of RV travel remains a constant source of adventure and exploration.

Reservations and permits

Recreational Vehicle (RV) travel has become increasingly popular in recent years, offering individuals and families the opportunity to explore the beauty of the great outdoors while enjoying the comforts of home on wheels. However, to ensure a smooth and enjoyable RV adventure, it's crucial to understand the importance of reservations and permits. Whether planning a cross- country road trip or a weekend getaway to a national park, having the right reservations and permits in place can make all the difference in your RV travel experience.

Reservations are essential to RV travel, especially when securing a spot at popular campgrounds and RV parks. Many campgrounds, especially those in high-demand areas, require advance reservations to guarantee a spot for your RV. These reservations can typically be made online or over the phone, and it's essential to plan well in advance, as some campgrounds book up months or even a year ahead of time. By making reservations, you ensure that you have a place to stay and avoid the stress and disappointment of arriving at a fully booked campground.

In addition to campgrounds, RV travelers should also consider reservations for RV parks and private campgrounds. While these options may not be as competitive as national parks, they often offer amenities such as full hookups, Wi-Fi, and entertainment options. Making reservations at RV parks can be especially crucial if you have specific requirements, such as access to a pool or pet-friendly accommodations. Having a reservation in place allows you to tailor your RV experience to your preferences and needs.

On the other hand, permits are essential for RV travel when exploring national parks, forests, and other protected areas. These permits are designed to regulate access and protect the environment while allowing visitors to enjoy these natural wonders responsibly. Before embarking on an RV adventure to a national park, it's crucial to research the specific permits required for the area you plan to visit. These permits can vary widely, depending on the park's location and the activities you intend to engage in, such as hiking, fishing, or wildlife viewing.

The entrance pass is one of the most common types of permits for RV travelers. This pass typically grants you access to a particular national park or recreational area for a specified period, usually seven days. It's essential to purchase these passes in advance, either online or at the park's entrance, to avoid delays and ensure you can enter the park. Many national parks also offer annual passes for frequent RV travelers, making it a cost-effective option for those planning multiple visits throughout the year.

In addition to entrance passes, some national parks require backcountry permits for RV travelers who want to explore more remote areas. These permits help park rangers track visitors' whereabouts, ensuring their safety and preserving the park's delicate ecosystems. If you plan to go off the beaten path in your RV, checking whether backcountry permits are necessary and obtaining them before starting your journey is crucial.

Another type of permit often required for RV travel is the camping permit. Many national parks and forests have designated campgrounds where RVs can park and set up camp. However, these campgrounds can fill up quickly, especially during the peak travel season. To secure a spot for your RV, it's essential to reserve a camping permit in advance. Some campgrounds may also have specific restrictions, such as maximum RV length or the number of nights you can stay, so be sure to review the campground's rules and regulations when making your reservation.

In conclusion, reservations and permits are indispensable aspects of RV travel, ensuring a safe and enjoyable journey. Reservations help you secure a spot at campgrounds and RV parks, allowing you to plan your trip confidently and conveniently. On the other hand, permits are essential when exploring national parks and protected areas, as they help regulate access and protect the environment. By understanding the importance of reservations and permits, RV travelers can embark on their adventures fully prepared and make the most of their time on the road. Whether you're a seasoned RV enthusiast or a first-time traveler, proper planning and compliance with reservation and permit requirements will undoubtedly enhance your RV travel experience.

Route planning and itineraries

Embarking on an RV adventure is an exhilarating experience, offering the freedom to explore new places while enjoying the comforts of home on wheels. However, effective route planning and itineraries are essential to make the most of your RV travel. These tools ensure a smoother journey and enhance the overall experience, allowing you to discover hidden gems, avoid pitfalls, and create lasting memories along the way.

The first step in planning an RV trip is to determine your destination. Whether you're dreaming of a cross-country road trip, a coastal expedition, or a visit to a specific destination, a clear goal is crucial. Once you've chosen your destination, the next step is to plan your route. Modern technology has made this task easier than ever, with GPS devices and navigation apps providing real-time traffic updates and alternative routes to avoid delays. However, having a paper map or an atlas on hand is essential as a backup, as technology can sometimes fail in remote areas or areas with poor signal reception.

Consider the distance you're comfortable driving in a day when planning your route. RV travel is meant to be enjoyable, and long hours behind the wheel can lead to fatigue and stress. Plan your stops strategically, aiming for a balance between driving and exploring. Many RV travelers find that limiting their daily drive to 200-300 miles allows for a more relaxed and enjoyable journey. This distance can vary depending on your preferences and the road conditions, so adjust it to suit your needs.

Incorporating rest stops, scenic detours, and attractions along your route can turn a simple journey into an unforgettable adventure. Research the places you'll pass through and identify points of interest that align with your interests. Whether it's visiting a national park, exploring a historic town, or indulging in local cuisine, planning these stops in advance can add depth to your travel experience. Moreover, RV travelers can use resources like travel guides, online forums, and mobile apps to discover hidden gems and recommendations from fellow travelers. When creating your itinerary, be sure to factor in overnight stays. Both public and private RV campgrounds are widely available across the country. Public campgrounds, managed by federal, state, and local agencies, often offer affordable options with basic amenities. On the other hand, private campgrounds provide a range of facilities, from full hookups to entertainment options like pools and recreational activities. Mixing both types of campgrounds in your itinerary is a good idea to balance convenience and budget.

Another crucial aspect of RV travel planning is to consider your chosen route's seasonal variations and weather conditions. Some areas may be inaccessible or less enjoyable during certain times of the year due to extreme weather conditions or road closures. Research your destination's climate and weather patterns and plan your trip accordingly. As unexpected weather changes or roadblocks can occur, flexibility is key, so have backup options and be prepared to adjust your itinerary as needed.

Safety is paramount when planning an RV trip, so be sure to perform regular maintenance checks on your RV before hitting the road. Ensure your vehicle is in good working condition, with functioning brakes, tires, and all necessary fluids topped off. Carry essential safety equipment, including fire extinguishers, first-aid kits, and tools for minor repairs. Additionally, check your insurance coverage to make sure you're adequately protected during your journey.

In conclusion, effective route planning and itineraries are fundamental to a successful RV travel experience. They provide a roadmap for your adventure, ensuring that you make the most of your journey and stay safe along the way. By choosing a destination, planning your route, considering your daily driving limits, incorporating interesting stops, and accounting for weather conditions, you can embark on an RV adventure that is not only enjoyable but also memorable. With the right planning and preparation, your RV travel experience can be a transformative journey filled with exploration, adventure, and cherished memories.

CHAPTER III

Hitting the Road

Preparing your RV for departure

Embarking on an RV adventure is an exciting endeavor, offering the opportunity to explore new destinations and create lasting memories with the comfort of a home on wheels. However, before you hit the road, ensuring that your RV is properly prepared for departure is crucial. Adequate preparation enhances safety and contributes to a smoother and more enjoyable journey. This section will explore the essential steps to take when getting your RV ready for the road.

First and foremost, it's essential to inspect your RV thoroughly. Start by checking the exterior for any signs of damage or wear and tear. Examine the tires for proper inflation, tread depth, and signs of damage. Check the brakes, lights, and signals to ensure they are functioning correctly. Inspect the roof for leaks or damage, and make any necessary repairs or maintenance. Additionally, check the awnings, windows, and doors to ensure they are in good working condition and properly sealed.

Moving inside your RV, perform a detailed inspection of the interior. Check all appliances, including the refrigerator, stove, oven, and microwave, to ensure they are in working order. Test the HVAC system to verify that both heating and cooling functions are operational. Check all plumbing systems, including faucets, toilets, and the water heater, for leaks or malfunctions. Ensure that all safety devices, such as smoke detectors and carbon monoxide detectors, are in good working condition.

Finally, inspect the interior for any signs of damage, including water stains or pest infestations, and address them promptly.

Next, it's essential to review your RV's documentation and ensure that all necessary paperwork is in order. This includes your RV's registration, insurance, and any required permits or licenses for the areas you plan to visit. Verify that your driver's license is up to date and valid in the states or countries you intend to travel through. Make photocopies of all essential documents and store them in a safe place, both in physical form and electronically, for easy access in case of emergencies.

One of the most critical aspects of RV preparation is ensuring that your vehicle is well-stocked and ready for the journey. Create a checklist of essential items, including kitchen supplies, bedding, toiletries, and entertainment options. Stock up on non-perishable food items, snacks, and bottled water to sustain you during your travels. Ensure that your RV's propane tanks are filled and that you have all the necessary adapters and hoses for hooking up to utilities at campgrounds. Pack any recreational equipment or gear you plan to use during your trip, such as bikes, kayaks, or fishing gear.

Safety should always be a top priority when preparing your RV for departure. Before hitting the road, conduct a safety briefing with all passengers on board. Review the location and operation of safety equipment, such as fire extinguishers, emergency exits, and seat belts. Establish a communication plan and designate a meeting point in case of separation. It's also advisable to have a first-aid kit readily available and familiarize yourself with its contents and use.

Routine maintenance is essential to keep your RV in optimal condition, and it's vital to perform necessary checks before departing. Ensure that the engine oil, transmission fluid, and other essential fluids are at the appropriate levels. Check the battery to ensure it is fully charged and in good condition. Lubricate moving parts, such as hinges and slides, to prevent excessive wear. Inspect the generator, if applicable, and make sure it is in working order.

Finally, don't forget to prepare for the unexpected. Carry a basic toolkit with essential tools and spare parts that may be needed for minor repairs on the road. Consider joining a roadside assistance program tailored explicitly for RVs to provide peace of mind in case of breakdowns or emergencies. Additionally, have a plan for waste disposal and understand how to use dump stations responsibly when necessary.

In conclusion, preparing your RV for departure is crucial in ensuring a safe and enjoyable travel experience. By conducting thorough inspections, reviewing documentation, stocking up on essentials, prioritizing safety, and performing routine maintenance, you can confidently set out on your RV adventure. Proper preparation not only enhances the reliability and functionality of your RV but also allows you to focus on the joy of the journey and the exploration of new horizons. With a well-prepared RV, you can embark on your adventure with peace of mind, ready to embrace the open road and all the experiences it offers.

Safety tips for RV travel

Recreational Vehicle (RV) travel is a fantastic way to explore the world's beauty while enjoying the comfort and convenience of a home on wheels. However, to ensure a safe and enjoyable RV adventure, it's crucial to prioritize safety at every step of the journey. From pre-departure preparations to on-the-road precautions, this section will provide you with essential safety tips for RV travel.

Before hitting the road, thorough pre-departure preparations are essential. Start by performing a comprehensive safety check of your RV. Inspect the exterior for any damage, including leaks, cracks, or loose parts. Check the tires for proper inflation, tread depth, and any signs of damage, such as cracks or punctures. Ensure that all lights, signals, and brakes are in working order. Take the time to inspect the propane system for leaks or loose connections, and make sure all appliances are functioning correctly. Conduct a test run of all safety equipment, including smoke detectors, carbon monoxide detectors, and fire extinguishers, to ensure they are operational.

Review your RV's documentation and ensure all necessary paperwork is in order. This includes up-to-date registration, insurance coverage, and any required permits or licenses for your travel destinations. Make photocopies of essential documents and store them in a safe place, both physically and electronically, for easy access in case of emergencies. Verify that your driver's license is valid for the states or countries you plan to visit and carry a spare set of keys for your RV.

Safety on the road begins with proper vehicle operation. RVs come in various sizes and configurations, and it's essential to be comfortable and confident in handling your specific vehicle. If you're new to RV travel, consider taking a driving course to learn the ropes and gain valuable skills. Be mindful of the RV's dimensions, especially its height and width, to avoid collisions with low-hanging branches, overpasses, or other obstacles. Keep a safe following distance from other vehicles to allow for the longer stopping distances required by RVs, and use your mirrors consistently to stay aware of your surroundings. It's

also crucial to plan your route with safety in mind. Research the roads you'll be traveling on and consider the conditions and terrain you may encounter. Some routes may have steep grades, narrow passages, or winding roads that require extra caution and slower speeds. Be aware of any weight restrictions or regulations that apply to your RV and adhere to them. Use a GPS or navigation app designed for RV travel to help you choose suitable routes and avoid low-clearance areas or other hazards.

Weather conditions can change rapidly, so staying informed and adapting your travel plans is essential. Monitor weather forecasts along your route and be prepared for adverse conditions, such as rain, snow, or high winds. If conditions become hazardous, consider delaying your travel or finding a safe place to wait until the weather improves. Driving in inclement weather can be challenging, so always prioritize safety over sticking to a strict schedule.

When it comes to parking and camping, choose your spots wisely. Look for well-maintained RV campgrounds and parks that offer essential amenities and security. Park your RV on level ground to ensure stability, and use leveling blocks if necessary. Be cautious when parking on uneven terrain or near bodies of water to avoid the risk of tipping or flooding. Always secure your RV with wheel chocks and stabilizers to prevent it from moving unexpectedly. Additionally, follow campground rules and guidelines, such as quiet hours and speed limits, to ensure a peaceful and safe stay for all.

Fire safety is a paramount concern during RV travel. Equip your RV with fire extinguishers in easily accessible locations and ensure everyone on board knows how to use them. Regularly check the smoke and carbon monoxide detectors to ensure they are in working condition and replace batteries as needed. Practice fire safety when cooking inside your RV; never leave stovetops or ovens unattended. Store flammable materials safely, away from heat sources, and have a designated meeting point for all occupants in case of an emergency evacuation.

Personal safety is equally crucial during RV travel. Be vigilant and aware of your surroundings, especially when staying in unfamiliar areas. Lock your RV doors and windows when you're not inside, and use additional security measures such as door wedge alarms or motion-sensor lights for added protection. Avoid displaying expensive items or valuables that may attract unwanted attention. If you're traveling alone, consider connecting with other RVers in the campground for a sense of community and safety.

Lastly, have a well-equipped RV emergency kit readily available. This kit should include essential items such as a first-aid kit, flashlights, batteries, an essential toolkit, road flares, a tire repair kit, and jumper cables. Familiarize yourself with how to use these tools and have a plan for dealing with common RV emergencies, such as flat tires or mechanical breakdowns.

In conclusion, safety should be the top priority for an RV adventure. From pre-departure checks to on-the-road precautions, taking the necessary steps to ensure the safety of yourself, your passengers, and your RV is essential. By following these safety tips, you can enjoy your RV travels with peace of mind, knowing that you are well-prepared to handle any situation that may arise.

Driving and navigation tips

Recreational Vehicle (RV) travel is a beautiful way to explore new destinations while enjoying the comforts of home on wheels. However, driving and navigating an RV can differ from driving a standard car or truck. Whether you're a seasoned RV enthusiast or a first-time traveler, you must be well-prepared and knowledgeable about the unique challenges and considerations that come with RV travel. This section will discuss important driving and navigation tips to ensure a safe and enjoyable RV journey.

First and foremost, it's crucial to become familiar with your RV's specifications and handling characteristics. RVs come in various sizes and types, from compact camper vans to large motorhomes, and each has its own set of driving nuances. Take the time to practice driving your RV in a safe and controlled environment, such as an empty parking lot, before hitting the open road. This practice will help you become comfortable with its size, turning radius, and braking distance.

One of the most significant differences between driving an RV and a regular vehicle is the increased size and weight of an RV. RVs are longer, taller, and heavier, which can affect their maneuverability and braking capabilities. It's crucial to maintain a safe following distance from other vehicles and anticipate the need for longer stopping distances. Give yourself extra space to react to changing traffic conditions, and avoid sudden lane changes or abrupt stops whenever possible.

When driving an RV, always be aware of your height clearance. Measure the height of your RV accurately, including any roof-mounted accessories like air conditioners or antennas. Low clearance areas, such as bridges, tunnels, and overpasses, can pose a significant hazard if you're unaware of your RV's height. Use navigation apps or GPS systems designed for RV travel to help you avoid routes with low clearances, and always obey height restriction signs.

In addition to height clearance, be cautious of weight limits and restrictions. Overloading your RV can lead to reduced stability, increased wear and tear on tires and brakes, and even accidents. Carefully distribute the weight of your belongings inside the RV and adhere to the manufacturer's recommended weight limits. Consider weighing your RV at a commercial truck scale to ensure you're within safe weight limits.

Another crucial aspect of RV travel is planning your route carefully. Not all roads are suitable for RVs, especially larger motorhomes. Research your route in advance and consider factors like road conditions, grades, and terrain. Steep inclines and declines can be challenging for RVs, particularly those towing additional vehicles or trailers. Choose routes with gentle grades and minimal elevation changes whenever possible.

Navigation apps and GPS devices designed for RV travel can be invaluable tools in planning your route. These systems consider your RV's size and weight, providing RV-friendly directions and helping you avoid hazards like low bridges or tight turns. Many of these devices also offer real-time traffic updates and alternative routes, allowing you to make adjustments as needed to avoid delays.

In addition to GPS navigation, having a paper map or atlas as a backup is essential. Technology can sometimes fail in remote areas or regions with poor signal reception. A physical map can be a lifesaver when you need to find your way or make route adjustments on the fly.

RV travelers should also consider the time of day when planning their driving schedule. Driving during daylight hours is generally safer, as visibility is better, and you can avoid the challenges of driving in the dark. It's also a good idea to plan your travel days with a balance between driving and rest stops. Long hours behind the wheel can lead to fatigue and decreased alertness, so aim for a maximum of 200-300 miles per day, allowing time for breaks and exploration.

When navigating within campgrounds or parking lots, exercise caution and patience. RVs have larger blind spots than regular vehicles, so use your mirrors and consider enlisting a spotter to help guide you when parking or maneuvering in tight spaces. Be courteous to fellow campers and follow campground rules and guidelines for safe driving and parking.

Lastly, always stay informed about weather conditions along your route. Weather can change rapidly, and being prepared for adverse conditions is essential. Monitor weather forecasts for your travel area and adjust your plans accordingly. In extreme weather, such as heavy rain, snow, or high winds, consider delaying your travel until conditions improve to ensure your safety on the road.

In conclusion, driving and navigation are fundamental aspects of RV travel that require special attention and considerations. By becoming familiar with your RV's handling characteristics, respecting height and weight limits, planning your route carefully, and using appropriate navigation tools, you can embark on your RV adventure with confidence and safety in mind. Remember to drive defensively, be aware of your surroundings, and adapt to changing conditions. With the right knowledge and precautions, RV travel can be a rewarding and enjoyable experience that allows you to explore the world while on the road.

Staying connected on the road

Recreational vehicle (RV) travel offers the allure of escaping the daily grind and immersing yourself in the beauty of the open road, but that doesn't mean you have to disconnect from the world completely. Staying connected while on an RV journey has become increasingly important in today's digital age. Whether it's for safety, work, or leisure, maintaining communication and internet access can enhance your RV travel experience. This section will explore various methods and tips for staying connected on the road during RV travel.

First and foremost, it's essential to have a reliable communication plan in place before embarking on your RV adventure. Ensure your mobile phone is in good working condition and has adequate coverage for the areas you plan to visit. Consider having a backup phone or a prepaid SIM card from a different carrier to ensure you have options in case of network issues. Additionally, let someone close to you know your travel itinerary and check-in regularly to provide updates on your location and well-being.

Internet access is often a top priority for many RV travelers, whether for work, entertainment, or staying in touch with loved ones. To ensure a seamless online experience, consider investing in a mobile hotspot device or a dedicated RV Wi-Fi solution. These devices allow you to create a private Wi-Fi network within your RV, providing internet connectivity for all your devices. Research different providers and plans to find one that suits your data usage needs and travel destinations.

Campgrounds and RV parks often offer Wi-Fi access, but the quality and reliability of these connections can vary widely. When choosing a campground, check if they provide Wi-Fi and inquire about its speed and coverage. Remember that campground Wi-Fi networks may become congested during peak times, affecting your internet speed. If staying connected is crucial, having your mobile hotspot or dedicated RV Wi-Fi can be more dependable. Another option for internet access on the road is utilizing your mobile phone's data plan for tethering. Most modern smartphones can act as mobile hotspots, allowing you to share your phone's cellular data connection with other devices like laptops or tablets. Be aware of your data plan's limitations and potential overage charges, as excessive data usage while tethering can quickly eat into your monthly data allotment.

Satellite internet is a more advanced and comprehensive option for staying connected in remote areas where traditional cellular coverage may be limited. RVers can install a satellite dish on their RV roof, providing high-speed internet access virtually anywhere in the country. However, satellite internet systems can be expensive to purchase and install, and ongoing monthly fees may also be substantial.

To maximize your connectivity on the road, consider using Wi-Fi signal boosters or extenders. These devices can enhance your RV's ability to receive and transmit Wi-Fi signals, even from a distance. Signal boosters can be particularly useful when you're parked in a campground with weak or spotty Wi-Fi coverage. Remember that these devices may require some technical setup and positioning to work effectively.

For those who need to work while traveling, creating a productive and comfortable workspace within your RV is essential. Invest in a reliable laptop with good battery life, ergonomic accessories like a keyboard and mouse, and noise-canceling headphones to minimize distractions. Designate a specific area in your RV for work to maintain a clear separation between work and leisure activities.

When it comes to staying connected for entertainment purposes, streaming services can be a great source of enjoyment during downtime. However, streaming video content consumes a significant amount of data, which can quickly deplete your data plan if you're not careful. Consider downloading movies or TV shows in advance while connected to Wi-Fi so that you can watch them offline without using data on the road.

Finally, don't forget about offline communication methods. While staying connected digitally is essential, having a plan for offline communication can be equally valuable. Carry a two-way radio or walkie-talkie for short-range communication with fellow travelers in areas with poor cellular reception. Additionally, having paper maps, an atlas, and a GPS navigation device or system as backups can help you find your way in case of technology failures.

In conclusion, staying connected on the road during RV travel is possible and increasingly accessible with modern technology. By planning ahead, investing in the right equipment and services, and being mindful of your data usage, you can enjoy a seamless online experience while exploring the beauty of the open road. Whether you're working remotely, staying in touch with loved ones, or simply enjoying entertainment on your journey, staying connected can enhance your RV travel experience and provide peace of mind in case of emergencies.

CHAPTER IV

National Park Essentials

Introduction to the National Park Service (NPS)

The United States is home to some of the world's most breathtaking natural landscapes and historical sites, many of which are preserved and protected by the National Park Service (NPS). Established in 1916, the NPS is a federal agency responsible for managing and conserving America's national parks, monuments, historic sites, and other designated areas of historical and natural significance. Its mission is to preserve these cherished places for the enjoyment of future generations while providing for their responsible use and stewardship. This section will delve into the history, mission, and significance of the National Park Service.

The National Park Service's roots can be traced back to the late 19th century when concerns about the conservation of America's natural wonders and historic treasures began to gain momentum. Influential figures like John Muir and Theodore Roosevelt advocated for preserving these areas and played key roles in raising awareness about the need for their protection. Under President Woodrow Wilson's administration, the NPS was officially established on August 25, 1916, with the passage of the National Park Service Organic Act.

The Organic Act defined the NPS's primary purpose as preserving national parks' natural and cultural resources "for the enjoyment, education, and inspiration of this and future generations." This legislation marked a significant milestone in the United States' conservation history, setting the stage for the protection and management of the nation's most valuable landscapes and historical sites. Today, the NPS manages over 400 units, including national parks, monuments, historic sites, seashores, and more, covering many ecosystems and historical periods.

The NPS is known for its commitment to preserving the nation's natural and cultural heritage through several key principles. Conservation lies at the heart of its mission, as the agency works tirelessly to safeguard fragile ecosystems, protect endangered species, and preserve the historic structures and artifacts that tell the story of America's past. This dedication to conservation goes hand in hand with providing opportunities for public enjoyment and recreation, ensuring that visitors can experience and appreciate these incredible places firsthand.

Education is another core aspect of the NPS's mission. National parks serve as living classrooms where visitors can learn about the geological, ecological, and historical features that make each area unique. The NPS strives to inspire a deeper understanding and appreciation of the natural world and American history through interpretive programs, visitor centers, guided tours, and informative signage.

In addition to education, the National Park Service strongly emphasizes research and science. It conducts research to monitor and protect the ecosystems and wildlife within national parks, as well as to understand better the cultural resources and historical significance of these areas. This scientific research informs park management decisions and contributes to our broader understanding of natural and cultural heritage.

One of the NPS's significant roles is the preservation of biodiversity. National parks are home to many ecosystems, from deserts and forests to wetlands and coastal environments. Within these diverse landscapes, the NPS manages and conserves a vast range of plant and animal species, many of which are threatened or endangered. Through careful management and conservation efforts, the NPS plays a critical role in protecting biodiversity and ensuring the survival of these species for generations to come.

The NPS is also responsible for preserving countless historic sites and cultural landmarks, including battlefields, forts, historic homes, and archaeological sites. These places provide insights into the nation's history and the people who shaped it. The NPS works diligently to protect and interpret these sites, allowing visitors to step back in time and gain a deeper appreciation for the events and individuals who have influenced the course of American history.

Every year, millions of visitors flock to national parks and other NPS-managed sites to explore their natural beauty, immerse themselves in history, and engage in outdoor recreation. The NPS has a robust network of facilities and services to accommodate these visitors, including campgrounds, hiking trails, visitor centers, and educational programs. While national parks are renowned for their grandeur, they also offer various recreational activities, from hiking and camping to birdwatching and stargazing.

The National Park Service faces several challenges in fulfilling its mission, including issues related to funding, climate change, and the increasing strain on park infrastructure due to high visitation. Addressing these challenges requires ongoing collaboration with partners, stakeholders, and the public. The NPS actively seeks public input and engagement to make informed decisions about park management and visitor experiences.

In conclusion, the National Park Service is vital in preserving America's natural and cultural heritage for present and future generations. With a mission deeply rooted in conservation, education, research, and public enjoyment, the NPS continues to protect and showcase the nation's most iconic landscapes and historical sites. Whether seeking adventure in the great outdoors or a deeper understanding of American history, national parks and NPS-managed areas offer something for everyone to enjoy and appreciate. As we celebrate the NPS's rich history and contributions to our nation, we also look forward to its ongoing commitment to preserving and sharing the wonders of the United States.

Park pass options

Visiting the stunning landscapes, historical sites, and natural wonders preserved within the National Park System is a rewarding experience for travelers of all interests. To make accessing these iconic destinations more convenient and cost-effective, the National Park Service (NPS) offers a variety of park pass options. These passes grant visitors access to national parks, monuments, and other federally managed recreation areas across the United States. This section will explore the different park pass options available to visitors and how they can enhance your national park experience.

The Annual Pass is a popular choice for frequent national park visitors. Priced reasonably, this pass offers unlimited entry to more than 2,000 federal recreation areas for an entire year from the date of purchase. It covers entrance fees for the pass holder and passengers in a single, private, non-commercial vehicle at sites that charge per vehicle. Additionally, the Annual Pass includes access to national forests, wildlife refuges, and other public lands managed by various federal agencies. Whether you plan to visit multiple national parks within a year or enjoy outdoor adventures on public lands, the Annual Pass is a cost-effective option.

The Senior Pass, available to U.S. citizens and permanent residents aged 62 and older, significantly discounts entrance fees to national parks and federal recreation areas. This lifetime pass offers unlimited access to these sites and covers the pass holder plus up to three accompanying adults in a non-commercial vehicle. Depending on the park's policies, the Senior Pass can also provide discounts on specific amenities, such as camping and guided tours. It's an excellent option for seniors who want to explore the nation's natural and cultural treasures at a reduced cost.

The Annual Pass for U.S. Military is a complimentary pass available to active-duty military personnel and their dependents. It grants free access to national parks, wildlife refuges, forests, and other federal lands. To obtain this pass, eligible military members can visit a participating federal recreation site in person and present their valid military ID. This pass offers a wonderful opportunity for military families to enjoy the great outdoors together without incurring entrance fees.

The Access Pass is designed to provide free lifetime access to U.S. citizens and permanent residents with permanent disabilities. Pass holders can enjoy complimentary entry to national parks and federal recreation areas, including discounts on some park amenities like camping. To obtain an Access Pass, individuals must provide documentation of their disability status, such as a statement from a licensed physician or a federal agency. This pass ensures that all visitors, regardless of their physical abilities, can explore the beauty and history of national parks.

The Every Kid Outdoors Pass aims to connect young people with the great outdoors by offering free access to national parks and federal lands for fourth-grade students and their families. This pass is part of an initiative to encourage outdoor exploration and environmental stewardship. Fourth-grade students can visit the Every Kid Outdoors website, complete an educational activity, and receive a paper pass that provides entry to participating sites. It's a fantastic way for families to introduce children to the wonders of nature and the importance of preserving our public lands.

In recognition of the valuable contributions of volunteers who dedicate their time and effort to national parks, the NPS offers several pass options for volunteers. These passes are typically provided to volunteers who accrue several service hours within a participating park or site. While the specific benefits of these passes may vary, they often include free entry to national parks and other federal recreation areas, making them a rewarding incentive for those who donate their time to help protect and preserve these special places.

Group Passes are available for organized groups, such as schools, scouts, and other educational or youth organizations. These passes offer free or reduced-cost entry to participating national parks and other federal lands for group members. Group leaders can obtain more information about eligibility and how to obtain group passes by contacting the specific park or site they plan to visit. Group Passes make engaging in outdoor learning and exploration easier for educational and youth groups.

In conclusion, the National Park Service offers a range of park pass options to accommodate visitors' diverse needs and interests. Whether you're a frequent national park enthusiast, a senior looking for affordable access, a military member or veteran, a person with disabilities, a fourth-grade student, a dedicated volunteer, or part of an organized group, there's likely a pass option tailored to your situation. These passes make visiting national parks more affordable and contribute to preserving and enjoying America's natural and cultural treasures. As you plan your next adventure, consider the park pass that best suits your circumstances, and embark on a journey of discovery and wonder in our nation's magnificent national parks and federal recreation areas.

Park rules and regulations

National parks, renowned for their awe-inspiring natural landscapes and cultural significance, attract millions of visitors annually. To safeguard these pristine environments and provide a safe and enjoyable experience for all, the National Park Service (NPS) has established a set of rules and regulations that govern visitor behavior and activities within national parks.

One of the fundamental rules in national parks is to stay on designated trails and pathways. These paths are thoughtfully planned to offer safe access to popular areas while minimizing environmental impact. Venturing off-trail can lead to ecological disruption, erosion, and harm to wildlife habitats. By remaining on established paths, visitors can appreciate the park's beauty without inadvertently causing harm.

The Leave No Trace principles are another essential set of guidelines. They promote responsible outdoor ethics, urging visitors to pack out all trash, properly dispose of waste, and minimize their environmental footprint. These principles encourage a "pack it in, pack it out" mentality, using designated restroom facilities, and adherence to park regulations regarding campfires and camping practices. Leave No Trace principles help ensure that natural and cultural resources remain unspoiled.

Respecting wildlife is a crucial rule in national parks. While encounters with wildlife are captivating, maintaining a safe distance and avoiding disturbances is paramount. Feeding wildlife is strictly prohibited, as it can disrupt natural behaviors and harm animals' health. Approaching or attempting to interact with wildlife can be dangerous for both humans and animals. Close-up views are best obtained through binoculars or telephoto lenses.

Campground regulations are vital to preserving the park environment and ensuring camper safety. These rules may include restrictions on campfire use, generator hours, and the maximum number of nights permitted in a campground. Proper food storage to prevent wildlife encounters is also crucial in some parks. Campers should familiarize themselves with specific park regulations and make reservations, if necessary, to ensure a seamless camping experience.

National parks welcome visitors with pets, but it's essential to adhere to pet regulations. Typically, pets must be kept on a leash and not allowed on trails or in certain sensitive areas. Cleaning up after pets and disposing of waste in designated receptacles is a must. Some parks offer specific pet-friendly trails and areas, so checking park-specific rules before bringing pets along is advisable.

Fire regulations are significant, especially in areas susceptible to wildfires. Campfires are subject to strict regulations, often requiring the use of designated fire rings and adherence to firewood restrictions. Visitors should always verify campfire regulations with park rangers and be prepared to use camp stoves for cooking when fires are prohibited.

Commercial activities within national parks, such as guided tours or photography workshops, may require special permits. These permits are necessary for any activity that involves a fee or provides services to the public. They help manage visitor use and maintain the quality and safety of commercial operations while safeguarding the park's resources.

Specific activities within national parks may necessitate special permits or reservations. These activities can include backcountry camping, river rafting, climbing, and more. Permits are issued to help park officials manage visitor use and protect sensitive areas. Visitors should consult with the park in advance and obtain any necessary permits to participate in these activities legally.

Drone use is regulated to protect visitor safety, maintain the natural soundscape, and preserve wildlife habitats. Drone use is generally prohibited within park boundaries, except for limited exceptions such as research and park management purposes. Visitors should leave drones at home or consult with park officials to understand specific regulations in a particular park.

National parks often have designated quiet hours and park hours. Quiet hours help maintain a peaceful atmosphere in campgrounds and public areas, while park hours ensure safe access to trails and viewpoints. Visitors should be aware of these hours and plan their activities accordingly.

In conclusion, national park rules and regulations are in place to protect the parks' natural and cultural treasures, ensure visitor safety, and provide a high-quality experience for all. Adhering to these rules and practicing responsible outdoor ethics helps preserve these extraordinary places for future generations to enjoy. Whether you're hiking, camping, or simply savoring the splendors of a national park, following these guidelines ensures that these remarkable environments will continue to inspire and captivate visitors for years to come.

Leave No Trace principles

Leave No Trace (LNT) is a set of principles and practices designed to promote responsible outdoor ethics and minimize human environmental impact when enjoying the great outdoors. These principles provide valuable guidelines for hikers, campers, and outdoor enthusiasts to ensure they leave nature as they found it, preserving its beauty and ecological integrity for future generations.

The first Leave No Trace principle emphasizes the importance of thorough planning before embarking on an outdoor adventure. This includes researching the chosen destination, understanding its regulations, and obtaining necessary permits. Adequate preparation also involves assessing your own skills and abilities, ensuring you have the appropriate gear, and considering factors like weather, group size, and the impact of your visit on the environment.

To minimize the impact of outdoor recreation, it is crucial to stay on established trails and camp in designated areas. Avoid trampling on fragile vegetation, disturbing wildlife, or creating new trails, as this can lead to soil erosion and damage ecosystems. Camping in designated areas with established fire rings and campsite amenities helps protect the environment and ensures that future generations can enjoy the same pristine landscapes. Proper waste disposal is a cornerstone of Leave No Trace principles. This means packing out all trash, litter, and food scraps from your outdoor excursions. Additionally, human waste must be dealt with responsibly. In areas where restroom facilities are available, use them. In more remote locations, use a portable toilet or dig a small, shallow hole at least 200 feet away from water sources to bury human waste.
Preserving the natural and cultural features of outdoor destinations is essential. Visitors should avoid picking plants, disturbing wildlife, or removing rocks, shells, or historical artifacts. Leave all natural and cultural resources as you found them so that others can experience the same sense of wonder and discovery. By respecting these features, we protect the integrity of ecosystems and ensure that future generations can appreciate their beauty and significance.

Campfires can be enjoyable but pose a significant environmental risk, especially in areas prone to wildfires. The Leave No Trace principles recommend using a camp stove for cooking to minimize the impact of campfires. If fires are permitted, use established fire rings or fire pans and burn only small sticks and twigs, keeping the fire small and under control. Be sure to adhere to park regulations regarding campfires and firewood collection.

Observing wildlife in its natural habitat can be a highlight of outdoor adventures, but it's essential to do so respectfully and without causing harm. Keep a safe distance from animals and never feed them, as human food can disrupt their natural behaviors and endanger their health. Use binoculars or a telephoto lens for close-up views and avoid approaching or attempting to interact with wildlife. Maintaining a respectful distance ensures both human safety and the well-being of animals.

Respect for fellow outdoor enthusiasts is a vital aspect of Leave No Trace principles. Keep noise levels to a minimum, yield the trail to others, and maintain a friendly and cooperative attitude. Keep group sizes manageable to minimize your impact on the environment and the experiences of others. Being considerate of fellow visitors, you help create a positive and harmonious outdoor experience for all.

Leave No Trace principles are not just guidelines for responsible outdoor recreation; they represent a commitment to environmental stewardship and preserving natural and cultural resources. Following these principles ensures that the beauty and integrity of our outdoor spaces are maintained, allowing current and future generations to enjoy them fully. Practicing Leave No Trace fosters a deeper connection to nature and promotes a sense of responsibility and respect for the environment. Whether you are an experienced outdoor enthusiast or a newcomer to outdoor adventures, embracing these principles can help make every outdoor experience more enjoyable, sustainable, and environmentally friendly. We can continue to cherish and protect the wilderness that enriches our lives by leaving no trace.

CHAPTER V

Making the Most of Your Park Visits

Selecting the best campgrounds

RV camping offers a unique blend of comfort and adventure, allowing travelers to explore the great outdoors while enjoying the convenience of a home on wheels. However, the success of your RV trip often hinges on the campground you choose. Selecting the right campground can significantly enhance your overall experience. In this section, we will explore the factors to consider when selecting the best campgrounds for RV camping.

Location is paramount when choosing a campground for RV camping. Consider your travel route and the attractions you wish to visit. Opt for campgrounds that are conveniently located near your intended destinations to minimize travel time and maximize your enjoyment. Many campgrounds provide easy access to national parks, hiking trails, lakes, and other outdoor attractions, making planning your trip around your interests and desired activities essential.

Determining your specific needs and preferences is critical to selecting a campground. RV campgrounds come in various types, each catering to different camping styles. Some campgrounds offer full hookups with water, electricity, and sewage connections, while others provide only partial hookups or dry camping options. Additionally, amenities such as Wi-Fi, laundry facilities, swimming pools, and pet-friendly accommodations vary from one campground to another. Assess your RV's requirements and your comfort preferences to choose a campground that aligns with your needs.

Another essential factor to consider is the size and type of your RV. Campgrounds may have limitations on the size and type of RV they can accommodate. Smaller campgrounds may not have the space for large Class A motorhomes, while some campgrounds cater exclusively to tent campers or smaller RVs. Ensure that the campground you select can comfortably accommodate your RV's size and length, and check for any restrictions or requirements regarding the type of RV allowed.

The camping season and weather conditions at your chosen destination play a vital role in selecting the best campground for your RV adventure. Some campgrounds are open year-round, while others operate seasonally. Research the climate and weather patterns for your travel dates to determine whether a campground will be suitable during your visit. In regions with extreme temperatures or frequent storms, choosing campgrounds with appropriate amenities, like electrical hookups for air conditioning or heating as needed is crucial.
Reservations are often essential for securing a spot at popular campgrounds, especially during peak travel seasons. Many campgrounds offer online reservation systems that allow you to book your RV site in advance. However, availability can fill up quickly, so making reservations well ahead of your planned travel dates is advisable. If you prefer flexibility and spontaneity, consider campgrounds that offer a mix of reservation and first-come, first-served sites.

Cost is an important consideration when selecting a campground for RV camping. Campground fees vary widely based on location, amenities, and services provided. Some campgrounds offer discounts for seniors, veterans, or members of camping clubs like Good Sam or KOA. Create a budget for your RV trip, considering campground fees, and factor in any additional costs for amenities and services you desire.

Campground reviews and recommendations from fellow RVers can provide valuable insights into the quality and suitability of campgrounds. Websites, forums, and social media groups dedicated to RV camping often feature reviews and personal experiences other travelers share. Reading these reviews can help you gauge past visitors' overall satisfaction and better understand what to expect at a campground.

Consider the atmosphere and ambiance you prefer when camping in your RV. Some campgrounds offer a serene and natural setting, while others provide a more social and community-oriented environment. Do you seek solitude and a connection with nature, or do you prefer campgrounds with organized activities and social gatherings? Determine the atmosphere that aligns with your camping style to choose a campground that offers the desired experience.

The availability of recreational opportunities is essential in selecting a campground for RV camping. Many campgrounds are situated near outdoor activities such as hiking, biking, fishing, and water sports. If you have specific activities in mind, choose a campground that offers convenient access to your preferred recreational opportunities. Additionally, consider the availability of trails, scenic viewpoints, and wildlife viewing opportunities within or near the campground.

In conclusion, selecting the best campgrounds for RV camping involves carefully assessing your needs, preferences, and travel plans. You can choose a campground that enhances your RV adventure by considering factors such as location, amenities, RV size and type, weather conditions, reservations, costs, reviews, ambiance, and recreational opportunities. The right campground can transform your RV trip into a memorable and enjoyable experience, allowing you to connect with nature, explore new destinations, and create lasting memories on the road.

Exploring Park visitor centers

One of the most rewarding aspects of RV camping is the opportunity to immerse yourself in national parks' natural beauty and cultural richness. These protected areas offer many experiences, from scenic vistas and wildlife encounters to historical sites and educational programs. To make the most of your RV camping adventure, consider exploring park visitor centers, which serve as gateways to the wonders of these natural treasures.

Visitor centers are often the first stop for RV campers when entering a national park. These facilities provide a wealth of information, including maps, brochures, and knowledgeable park rangers who can answer questions and offer recommendations. Visitor centers are invaluable for planning your itinerary, understanding park regulations, and staying informed about current conditions, such as weather alerts or trail closures. They serve as a hub for gathering essential details to enhance your RV camping experience.

One of the primary benefits of visiting a park's visitor center is gaining insight into the park's natural and cultural history. Most centers feature informative exhibits, displays, and audiovisual presentations illuminating the park's unique features, geology, flora, and fauna. These exhibits provide a deeper understanding of the park's ecological significance, making your RV camping trip enjoyable and educational. Visitors of all ages can appreciate these centers' fascinating stories and natural wonders.

Park ranger programs and guided tours are frequently organized through visitor centers, offering immersive experiences that enhance your RV camping adventure. These programs may include guided hikes, wildlife watching, astronomy programs, or cultural demonstrations. Participating in these activities allows you to delve deeper into the park's offerings and personally connect with its natural and cultural heritage. Park rangers and guides are passionate about sharing their knowledge and helping visitors forge meaningful connections with the park.

Many visitor centers also offer interactive exhibits and educational materials tailored to children and families. These resources engage young explorers in the wonders of the natural world while teaching them about conservation and environmental stewardship. Junior Ranger programs, available at most national parks, allow children to complete activities, earn badges, and become advocates for protecting our natural resources. RV camping with children becomes a more enriching experience when you take advantage of these educational opportunities.

In addition to educational resources, visitor centers often provide practical amenities for RV campers. Restrooms, drinking water, and picnic areas are commonly available, ensuring you can comfortably enjoy your visit. Some visitor centers even offer gift shops where you can purchase souvenirs, books, and maps to commemorate your RV camping adventure. These amenities enhance your overall comfort and convenience during your park exploration.

For those seeking outdoor adventures, visitor centers are excellent starting points for accessing hiking trails, scenic viewpoints, and other recreational opportunities within the park. Rangers and staff can advise on the best trails for your skill level and interests, recommend safety precautions, and provide up-to-date information on trail conditions. Whether you're a seasoned hiker or a novice explorer, visitor centers help you embark on unforgettable journeys into the park's wilderness.

Visitor centers are also crucial in promoting responsible outdoor ethics and conservation. They offer information on Leave No Trace principles and educate visitors about the importance of protecting fragile ecosystems. By following these guidelines, RV campers can minimize their environmental impact and contribute to the long-term preservation of these natural wonders. Visitor centers serve as advocates for sustainability and responsible tourism within national parks.

In conclusion, exploring park visitor centers is an integral part of the RV camping experience in national parks. These centers offer a wealth of resources, educational opportunities, and practical amenities that enhance your adventure. Whether you're seeking information, guided programs, interactive exhibits, or outdoor adventures, visitor centers serve as invaluable gateways to the wonders of the natural world. By visiting these facilities during your RV camping trip, you'll gain a deeper appreciation for the parks you explore and create lasting memories that connect you to the natural and cultural heritage of these remarkable destinations.

Participating in ranger-led programs

RV camping allows outdoor enthusiasts to immerse themselves in the beauty of national parks and explore the wonders of the natural world while enjoying the comfort of a home on wheels. While independent exploration is a significant part of RV camping, participating in ranger-led programs is an often overlooked and highly rewarding aspect of the experience. These programs, led by knowledgeable park rangers, offer an opportunity to gain deeper insights into national parks' natural and cultural wonders while connecting with like-minded travelers. This section will explore the benefits and advantages of participating in ranger-led programs on an RV camping trip.

Ranger-led programs come in various forms, each tailored to showcase a particular national park's unique features and resources. These programs may include guided hikes, wildlife viewing excursions, stargazing events, historical reenactments, and cultural demonstrations. Park rangers are experts in their respective fields and passionate about sharing their knowledge and love for the outdoors. Their enthusiasm adds depth and authenticity to their experiences, making ranger-led programs both educational and enjoyable.

One of the primary benefits of participating in ranger-led programs is the opportunity to learn about the park's natural and cultural history from experts intimately familiar with its resources. Rangers often incorporate storytelling, demonstrations, and hands-on activities to engage participants and bring the park's history to life. Whether you're interested in the geology of the landscape, the behavior of local wildlife, the traditions of indigenous cultures, or the tales of early explorers, ranger-led programs provide a rich and immersive learning experience.

Ranger-led programs cater to various interests and skill levels, making them accessible to RV campers of all backgrounds and ages. Families with children can enjoy programs designed specifically for young explorers, where kids can earn Junior Ranger badges by completing activities and learning about the park's natural and cultural heritage. For more experienced adventurers, programs may include challenging hikes to remote areas, birdwatching expeditions, or in-depth discussions about specific scientific research projects taking place within the park.

Participating in ranger-led programs enhances your overall understanding of the park's ecosystems and conservation efforts. Rangers often address topics such as wildlife management, the importance of preserving native habitats, and the challenges posed by climate change. This knowledge fosters a greater appreciation for the natural world and empowers RV campers to advocate for responsible outdoor ethics and conservation. By learning how to minimize their impact on the environment through Leave No Trace principles, participants can contribute to protecting these natural treasures.

Another advantage of ranger-led programs is the opportunity to explore park areas that may be less accessible to the general public. Rangers often lead guided hikes to remote or restricted locations, providing participants with a unique and memorable experience. These excursions may include visits to pristine wilderness areas, secluded waterfalls, or historical sites not typically open to independent exploration. Such opportunities allow RV campers to delve deeper into the park's hidden gems and create lasting memories.

Safety and preparedness are paramount in national parks, and ranger-led programs prioritize these aspects. Rangers are trained to assess environmental conditions, manage risks, and ensure the safety of program participants. Whether you're embarking on a backcountry hike or attending an evening astronomy program, rangers provide valuable guidance and safety tips to enhance your enjoyment and minimize potential hazards. This expertise allows RV campers to engage in outdoor adventures with confidence.

Participating in ranger-led programs also allows connecting with fellow RV campers and sharing experiences with like-minded individuals. These programs often attract people with a passion for the outdoors and a curiosity about the park's resources. Engaging in group activities, discussing shared interests, and exchanging stories with fellow participants can lead to meaningful connections and the formation of lasting friendships, enriching your RV camping journey.

Lastly, ranger-led programs can provide a more profound sense of fulfillment and connection to the national parks you visit. These experiences foster a profound appreciation for these protected areas' natural and cultural heritage and create a sense of responsibility for their preservation. By actively engaging with park rangers and fellow participants, you become a part of the park's ongoing story, contributing to its conservation and ensuring that future generations can enjoy these treasured landscapes.

In conclusion, participating in ranger-led programs on an RV camping trip offers many benefits that enhance your overall experience in national parks. These programs provide educational, enjoyable, and safe opportunities to explore these protected areas' natural and cultural wonders. By learning from passionate and knowledgeable park rangers, connecting with fellow RV campers, and immersing yourself in the park's history and resources, you can create unforgettable memories and develop a profound appreciation for the beauty and significance of our national parks. Whether you're a seasoned outdoor enthusiast or new to RV camping, ranger-led programs offer enriching experiences that add depth and meaning to your adventures in these remarkable destinations.

Choosing and planning hikes

RV camping provides the perfect opportunity to explore the beauty and serenity of national parks and other natural destinations while enjoying the comforts of home on wheels. A significant component of RV camping is embarking on hikes that allow you to immerse yourself in the great outdoors. However, selecting and planning hikes on an RV camping trip requires careful consideration to ensure a safe, enjoyable, and rewarding experience. This section will explore the essential aspects of choosing and planning hikes during your RV camping adventure.

The first step in choosing a hike for your RV camping trip is to consider your fitness level and hiking experience. Hikes range from easy, family-friendly strolls to challenging backcountry excursions. Assess your fellow travelers' physical capabilities and abilities to determine the appropriate difficulty level for your group. Selecting a hike that matches your fitness level ensures a more enjoyable and manageable experience.

Once you've assessed your fitness level, research the trails available in the national park or natural area where you're RV camping. Most parks provide trail maps, descriptions, and information about each trail's distance, elevation gain, and estimated hiking time. Review these resources to identify hikes that align with your preferences and capabilities. Pay attention to the trail's features, such as scenic viewpoints, waterfalls, or historical sites, as these can enhance your hiking experience.

Weather and seasonality play a crucial role in hike planning. Different trails may be more suitable during specific times of the year due to weather conditions, trail closures, or seasonal factors like wildflower blooms or fall foliage. Before setting out on a hike, check the current weather forecast for the area and verify trail conditions with park rangers or visitor centers. Being prepared for changing weather conditions ensures your safety and comfort while on the trail.

When planning hikes on an RV camping trip, having the right gear and equipment is essential. Comfortable, moisture-wicking clothing, sturdy hiking boots or shoes, a backpack, a map and compass or GPS device, sunscreen, insect repellent, and plenty of water are some of the essential items you should include in your hiking gear. Depending on the hike's difficulty and duration, you may also need additional items such as trekking poles, first aid supplies, and a headlamp. Proper gear ensures you are well-prepared for any challenges you may encounter on the trail.

Safety is a top priority when selecting and planning hikes during your RV camping adventure. Always inform someone of your hiking plans, including the trail you intend to take, your estimated return time, and any emergency contact information. This precaution allows for a quicker response in case of an unexpected situation. It's also advisable to hike with a buddy or in a group, as companions can provide assistance and support if needed. If you're RV camping alone, let someone at your campground know about your hiking plans.

Trail etiquette and Leave No Trace principles are essential considerations when planning hikes on an RV camping trip. Stay on designated trails to minimize environmental impact and prevent trail erosion. Yield the trail to hikers going uphill, and be courteous to fellow hikers and wildlife. Carry out all trash and litter, and dispose of it properly at the campground or visitor center. Follow Leave No Trace principles to ensure that the area's natural beauty remains unspoiled for future generations to enjoy.

Hiking with a purpose can add depth to your RV camping adventure. Consider incorporating nature appreciation, wildlife observation, or photography elements into your hikes. Carry a field guide or binoculars to identify plants and animals, or bring along a camera to capture the breathtaking scenery. Engaging with the natural world on a more profound level allows you to connect with the environment and create lasting memories.

While planning hikes on an RV camping trip, be flexible with your schedule and expectations. Weather conditions, trail closures, or unexpected events can alter your plans. It's essential to have alternative hike options or backup activities in case your initial choice is unavailable.

Additionally, be mindful of your physical condition during a hike. If you encounter challenging terrain or unexpected fatigue, don't hesitate to turn back or modify your plans to ensure your safety and well-being.

One of the joys of RV camping is returning to the comfort of your campsite after a day of hiking. Before heading out on a hike, ensure you have a sufficient supply of food, snacks, and water for your return. Consider packing a picnic lunch to enjoy at a scenic viewpoint or a shady spot along the trail. Rest and replenish your energy before returning to your RV, where you can relax, cook a hearty meal, and reflect on the day's adventures.

In conclusion, choosing and planning hikes on an RV camping trip is essential to the overall experience. You can ensure a rewarding and enjoyable hiking adventure by carefully considering factors such as your fitness level, trail difficulty, weather conditions, and safety measures. Hiking allows you to connect with the natural world, appreciate the beauty of the outdoors, and create lasting memories during your RV camping journey. With proper planning and preparation, you can embark on hikes that enhance your connection to nature and enrich your RV camping adventure.

CHAPTER VI

RV Camping in National Parks

Campground options within parks

Recreational Vehicle (RV) camping has become an increasingly popular way for people to connect with nature while enjoying the comforts of home on the road. For those looking to experience the great outdoors within the confines of national and state parks, numerous campground options are designed specifically for RV enthusiasts. These campgrounds offer a unique blend of natural beauty, convenience, and community, making them a top choice for outdoor enthusiasts.

One of the most appealing aspects of RV camping in parks is the diversity of campgrounds available. Parks often offer a range of options to cater to various preferences and needs. Full-hookup sites are a favorite among RVers, providing electricity, water, and sewer connections. This level of convenience ensures that campers can enjoy all the amenities of home, such as air conditioning, hot showers, and kitchen appliances, while still immersing themselves in the natural surroundings. Partial-hookup and primitive sites are also common, allowing campers to choose their desired level of comfort and self-sufficiency.

The selection of campgrounds within parks allows campers to tailor their experience to their desired level of immersion in nature. Some campgrounds are situated deep within the wilderness, providing a true escape from civilization. These campgrounds often lack modern amenities, encouraging campers to rely on their resources and survival skills. On the other hand, there are campgrounds near visitor centers and other facilities, offering a more convenient experience with access to information, guided tours, and even campfire programs. This variety ensures that every RV camper can find the perfect spot to suit their preferences.

In addition to location and amenities, campground options within parks also vary in size and capacity. Some campgrounds are smaller, with fewer sites, creating a more intimate and peaceful atmosphere. These campgrounds are ideal for those seeking solitude and a closer connection with nature. Larger campgrounds, on the other hand, can accommodate more campers and tend to have a livelier atmosphere. This can particularly appeal to families and social RV groups seeking a sense of community during outdoor adventure.

One noteworthy aspect of RV camping in parks is the stunning natural beauty that often surrounds these campgrounds. Many parks are home to breathtaking landscapes like mountains, lakes, forests, and canyons. RV campers can wake up to magnificent views right outside their windows and step outside to explore the wonders of the natural world. Whether it's watching the sunrise over a pristine lake or stargazing under a clear, starry sky, the beauty of these campgrounds enhances the overall camping experience.

Furthermore, the campground options within parks frequently offer various recreational activities and opportunities for adventure. Hiking trails, wildlife viewing, fishing, and water activities are just a few of the possibilities awaiting campers. Some parks even provide interpretive programs and ranger-led activities, allowing visitors to learn more about the park's history, geology, and ecology. This combination of outdoor recreation and educational experiences makes RV camping in parks a well-rounded adventure for nature enthusiasts of all ages.

Another advantage of camping in parks is the sense of community that often develops among RV campers. Sharing a campground with like-minded individuals who share a passion for the outdoors can lead to lasting friendships and memorable experiences. Campfires, cookouts, and group activities are common occurrences in these campgrounds, fostering a sense of camaraderie that enhances the overall enjoyment of the trip. This communal aspect of RV camping within parks adds a unique dimension to the camping experience.

In conclusion, RV camping within parks offers a diverse range of campground options, each with its own set of advantages and unique experiences. Whether campers seek full-hookup sites with modern amenities, remote wilderness locations, or a sense of community, a campground meets their needs. The natural beauty, recreational opportunities, and the potential for meaningful connections with fellow campers make RV camping in parks an exceptional way to experience the great outdoors. As more people discover the joys of RV camping, these campgrounds continue to be a beloved choice for those seeking adventure, relaxation, and a deeper connection with the natural world.

Reservations vs. first-come, first-served

When embarking on an RV camping adventure, one of the crucial decisions that campers must make is whether to opt for campgrounds that offer reservations or those that operate on a first-come, first-served basis. Both options have their own set of advantages and disadvantages, and choosing between them largely depends on individual preferences, flexibility, and the type of camping experience one seeks.

Reservations have become increasingly popular in the world of RV camping due to the convenience and peace of mind they offer. With a reservation, campers can secure a specific campsite for a set date, eliminating the worry of arriving at a campground only to find all sites occupied. This option is especially appealing during peak camping seasons when campgrounds tend to be crowded, as it guarantees a spot and allows for better planning.

Reservations also allow campers to choose their desired amenities and location within the campground. Whether it's a full-hookup site, a lakeside view, or proximity to restroom facilities, making a reservation ensures that campers get the campsite that best suits their needs and preferences. This level of control can significantly enhance the overall camping experience, allowing for a more tailored and comfortable stay.

On the flip side, first-come, first-served campgrounds offer a sense of spontaneity and adventure that appeals to many RV enthusiasts. Campers who choose this option are often willing to take the risk of arriving at a campground without a reservation, hoping to find an available site. This approach can be advantageous when campers discover hidden gems or snag prime sites that were vacated by early morning departures.

First-come, first-served campgrounds also foster a greater sense of community among campers. Since everyone arrives without a pre-assigned site, there's a camaraderie that develops as campers help each other locate available spaces and share information about the best spots. This communal aspect of first-come, first-served camping can lead to unexpected friendships and memorable social interactions.

Flexibility is another crucial factor to consider when deciding between reservations and first-come, first-served campgrounds. Reservations offer certainty and peace of mind but require campers to adhere to a fixed schedule. Campers must arrive on the designated date and occupy their reserved site, which may limit the ability to stay longer if they wish. In contrast, first-come, first-served campgrounds offer greater flexibility regarding arrival and departure dates. Campers can extend their stay if they find the campground to be a perfect fit or move on to a new destination without prior commitments.

Cost can also play a role in the decision-making process. Reservations typically require an upfront fee to secure a campsite, and this cost can vary depending on the campground and the amenities offered. In contrast, first-come, first-served campgrounds often require campers to pay upon arrival, allowing for more flexibility in budgeting and decision-making.

It's important to note that the availability of reservations or first-come, first-served options can vary from one campground to another. Some campgrounds exclusively offer one of these options, while others may have a mix of both. Campers should research their desired destination in advance to understand the booking policies and availability.

In conclusion, the choice between reservations and first-come, first-served campgrounds ultimately depends on individual preferences and the type of RV camping experience one seeks. Reservations provide convenience, peace of mind, and the ability to plan ahead, while first-come, first-served campgrounds offer spontaneity, a sense of adventure, and a unique sense of community. Flexibility and budget considerations also play a role in the decision-making process. Regardless of the choice made, RV camping offers the opportunity to connect with nature and enjoy the great outdoors, making it a memorable and rewarding experience.

RV hookups and amenities

Recreational Vehicle (RV) camping has evolved significantly over the years, with modern RVs offering a wide range of amenities to ensure a comfortable and enjoyable camping experience. One of the key elements that contribute to the convenience of RV camping is the availability of RV hookups and amenities at campgrounds. These hookups provide essential utilities, allowing RVers to enjoy the comforts of home while exploring the great outdoors.

RV hookups typically encompass three main categories: water, electricity, and sewer. These utilities are essential for ensuring a seamless and enjoyable camping experience. Water hookups provide a direct water supply to the RV, allowing campers to have a consistent source of fresh water for cooking, cleaning, and bathing. Electricity hookups, often called "shore power," provide the RV with a reliable electrical power source. This allows campers to run appliances, charge electronic devices, and maintain a comfortable interior climate with heating or air conditioning.

Sewer hookups, also known as "dump stations" or "sewer connections," are crucial for managing waste disposal from the RV's bathroom facilities. They allow campers to directly connect their RV's sewer system to the campground's sewage infrastructure. This eliminates the need to constantly empty holding tanks, providing a more convenient and hygienic solution for waste management.

In addition to these fundamental hookups, many campgrounds offer various levels of amenities to enhance the RV camping experience. As the name suggests, full-hookup sites provide all three essential utilities: water, electricity, and sewer. These sites are highly sought after by RVers because they offer the convenience of home on the road. Campers can use all of their RV's amenities without worrying about resource limitations.

Partial-hookup sites, on the other hand, may offer only some of the utilities. For instance, a site might provide water and electricity but lack sewer connections. While these sites may require more conservative water and waste management, they still offer significant convenience for RV campers.

Some campgrounds also offer "dry camping" or "boondocking" sites with no hookups. Dry camping requires campers to rely solely on the resources within their RV, such as onboard water tanks and batteries. While this option provides a more rustic and self-sufficient experience, it also necessitates careful planning and conservation of resources.

Beyond hookups, amenities at RV campgrounds can vary widely. Many campgrounds provide additional facilities such as restrooms, showers, and laundry facilities. These amenities can be especially valuable for RVers who want to conserve their onboard resources or simply enjoy the convenience of using campground facilities.

Moreover, campgrounds often feature recreational amenities to enhance the camping experience. These may include swimming pools, playgrounds, hiking trails, picnic areas, and even Wi-Fi access. Such amenities allow campers to relax and enjoy their time outdoors while staying connected and entertained.

Campground size and layout also play a role in the camping experience. Some campgrounds are nestled in natural settings with spacious, wooded sites providing privacy and a sense of natural immersion in nature. Others are designed with a more social atmosphere in mind, featuring closer proximity between sites and communal areas for gatherings and activities.

It's worth noting that the availability of RV hookups and amenities can vary from one campground to another. State and national parks, for instance, may have limited or no hookups, prioritizing a more rustic experience. On the other hand, private campgrounds and RV resorts tend to offer a wider range of amenities, making them a popular choice for RVers seeking a comfortable and well-equipped camping environment.

In conclusion, RV hookups and amenities have revolutionized the camping experience, allowing RVers to enjoy the conveniences of home while exploring the great outdoors. Water, electricity, and sewer hookups are essential for a seamless camping experience, while amenities such as restrooms, showers, and recreational facilities enhance the overall enjoyment of the trip. Whether campers prefer a full-hookup site with all the comforts of home or a more rustic experience in a dry camping setting, RV hookups and amenities provide options for a diverse range of camping preferences. RV camping continues to offer the perfect balance between adventure and comfort, making it a popular choice for outdoor enthusiasts of all kinds.

Boondocking and dry camping

In RV camping, two terms often come up are "boondocking" and "dry camping." These terms refer to camping without established campgrounds' traditional hookups and amenities. Boondocking and dry camping offer a more rustic and self-sufficient camping experience, allowing RVers to connect with nature and enjoy a sense of freedom and adventure that is distinct from camping in established campgrounds.

Boondocking, sometimes referred to as "wild camping" or "off-grid camping," is the practice of camping in remote or undeveloped areas without traditional campground amenities. This means RVers are entirely self-reliant and must bring everything they need, from water and electricity to waste management solutions. Boondocking locations can range from secluded spots deep in the wilderness to more accessible areas on public lands like Bureau of Land Management (BLM) or U.S. Forest Service lands. What sets boondocking apart is the opportunity to camp in truly unspoiled natural settings.

One of the primary appeals of boondocking is the sense of solitude and connection with nature it offers. Breathtaking landscapes, serene lakes, majestic mountains, and pristine forests can surround campers who choose this camping style. The absence of crowds and campground noise allows for a deep immersion in the natural environment, providing a unique opportunity to appreciate the beauty of the great outdoors.

While boondocking may lack traditional hookups, it often rewards campers with unparalleled tranquility and a sense of adventure. RVers can take advantage of their self-contained systems, such as onboard water tanks, generators, and solar panels, to maintain a comfortable and functional living space. Many RVers who embrace boondocking develop energy conservation and resource management skills, making them more self-sufficient and environmentally conscious.

On the other hand, dry camping typically involves camping in designated areas that may lack traditional hookups but provide some level of basic amenities. These areas can include state or national forest campgrounds, Bureau of Land Management sites, or even some parking lots and rest areas. While dry camping may not offer all the comforts of home, it often includes features like picnic tables, fire rings, and access to vault toilets or pit toilets.

Dry camping can be an excellent option for RVers who want a bit more convenience and a sense of security compared to boondocking in the wilderness. It strikes a balance between self-sufficiency and access to basic facilities. Campers still need to rely on their RV's onboard resources and may need to conserve water and electricity, but they can enjoy a more structured and accessible camping experience.

Both boondocking and dry camping offer unique advantages. Boondocking provides a deeper connection to nature and a more remote and adventurous experience, while dry camping offers a level of comfort and convenience without the crowds and amenities of established campgrounds. However, both styles of camping require careful planning and preparation.

Before embarking on a boondocking or dry camping adventure, RVers should consider several essential factors. First and foremost, they need to ensure their RV is equipped with the necessary resources to handle the demands of self-contained camping. This includes having sufficient water storage, energy sources (such as generators or solar panels), and waste management solutions (like portable waste tanks).

Researching and selecting appropriate camping locations is also crucial. RVers should be aware of the regulations and rules governing camping on public lands, as well as any permit requirements. Additionally, they should be prepared for the absence of cell phone reception and limited access to services, which can be common when camping in remote areas.

Furthermore, campers must practice responsible and sustainable camping practices. This includes Leave No Trace principles, which emphasize minimizing environmental impact by properly disposing of waste, using established fire rings, and respecting the natural surroundings. Maintaining a low impact ensures that these beautiful wilderness areas remain pristine for future generations to enjoy.

In conclusion, boondocking and dry camping allow RVers to embrace a more rugged and self-reliant camping experience. Boondocking, in particular, offers a deeper connection to nature and a sense of adventure that can be truly rewarding. Dry camping balances convenience and self-sufficiency, making it an attractive option for those who want a structured camping experience without traditional hookups. Regardless of the choice, campers should be well-prepared, practice responsible camping, and embrace the freedom and beauty that come with these off-grid camping styles. Boondocking and dry camping continue to be cherished by RV enthusiasts seeking to escape the hustle and bustle of modern life and find solace in the great outdoors.

CHAPTER VII

Outdoor Activities

Hiking and backpacking

RV camping is a fantastic way to explore the great outdoors while enjoying the comforts of home on the road. While many RV enthusiasts relish in RVs' convenience and relaxation, they also appreciate the opportunity to engage in outdoor activities that bring them closer to nature. Among these activities, hiking and backpacking are popular choices for RV campers looking to explore their surroundings' natural beauty and serenity.

Hiking is a versatile outdoor activity that can be easily incorporated into an RV camping trip. Many public or private campgrounds are situated near or within national or state parks, forests, or wilderness areas. These locations often offer a network of hiking trails that cater to hikers of various skill levels, making it accessible for beginners and experienced trekkers alike.

One of the significant advantages of hiking during an RV camping trip is the opportunity to immerse oneself in the natural environment. Hikers can traverse trails that wind through lush forests, climb mountains, follow rivers, or lead to scenic overlooks. These experiences allow campers to witness the breathtaking beauty of landscapes that might not be accessible by vehicle alone. The sights, sounds, and smells of the wilderness come to life as hikers venture deeper into nature.

Hiking also provides a sense of adventure and exploration. RVers can choose from various trails with varying lengths and difficulty levels, ensuring a hike suitable for everyone in the group. Whether it's a leisurely stroll along a nature trail or a challenging ascent to a summit, each hike offers a unique adventure waiting to be discovered. Many campers find that hiking becomes an integral part of their RV camping experience, as it provides a deeper connection to the natural world and offers a refreshing break from the daily routine.

Backpacking takes the experience of hiking to a more immersive level. While hiking typically involves day trips, backpacking allows campers to venture deeper into the wilderness by carrying all their necessities in a backpack and camping overnight along the trail. RV campers looking to combine their love for RVing with backpacking can embark on "basecamp" backpacking adventures, where the RV serves as the home base, and day hikes or multi-day backpacking trips radiate out from there.

Backpacking adds an element of self-sufficiency and self-reliance to the camping experience. Campers must carefully plan and pack all the essentials, including food, water, shelter, and safety gear, before setting out on their backpacking adventure. This level of preparedness ensures that backpackers are self-sustained while exploring remote and pristine wilderness areas.

Moreover, backpacking offers the opportunity to experience the tranquility and solitude of the wilderness like no other activity. Campers can choose less frequented trails, allowing for a deeper connection with nature and a sense of peace and serenity that can be hard to find in more populated areas. The absence of modern distractions and the simplicity of life on the trail can be a refreshing and rejuvenating experience for RV campers.

While backpacking presents its own set of challenges, such as carrying a heavy load and navigating rugged terrain, the rewards are well worth the effort. Campers often describe the sense of accomplishment and feeling truly connected to nature as the highlights of their backpacking adventures. The ability to camp under a star- filled sky, far away from the lights of civilization, is an experience that many RVers cherish.

It's essential for RV campers who plan to incorporate hiking or backpacking into their trips to be adequately prepared. Proper hiking or backpacking gear, including sturdy footwear, appropriate clothing, navigation tools, and safety equipment, is essential. Campers should also research their chosen trails, understand the terrain and weather conditions, and notify someone of their plans in an emergency.

In conclusion, hiking and backpacking are two outdoor activities that can significantly enhance the RV camping experience. Whether it's a leisurely hike on a scenic trail or an immersive backpacking adventure, these activities allow RV campers to connect with nature, explore the beauty of the wilderness, and enjoy the tranquility of the great outdoors. RV camping provides the perfect base from which to embark on these adventures, offering the comforts and conveniences of home while enabling campers to explore the world beyond their campsite. For those seeking a deeper connection with nature and a sense of adventure during their RV camping trips, hiking and backpacking are ideal.

Wildlife watching

One of the most rewarding aspects of RV camping is connecting with nature and observing wildlife in their natural habitats. Whether you're parked in a national park, nestled in a forest, or by the shore of a tranquil lake, wildlife is often just outside your RV door. Wildlife watching during RV camping is a favorite pastime for outdoor enthusiasts, offering a chance to witness the wonders of the natural world up close and personal.

One of the critical advantages of wildlife watching during RV camping is the convenience it provides. Many campgrounds and RV parks are strategically located in areas known for their biodiversity. These locations often have designated wildlife viewing areas, hiking trails, or even wildlife blinds where campers can observe animals in their natural habitats without venturing too far from their campsite. This convenience allows RV campers to enjoy wildlife encounters without requiring extensive travel or dedicated wildlife excursions.

The variety of wildlife that can be observed during RV camping is extensive. From birds to mammals, reptiles to amphibians, and insects to marine life, a wide range of species are waiting to be discovered. Birdwatching is a popular form of wildlife watching, with campers often spotting eagles, hawks, owls, and a diverse array of songbirds. Mammals such as deer, elk, foxes, and even bears are frequently encountered in forested areas and national parks. Coastal RV campers may have the chance to spot dolphins, seals, and whales, while those near bodies of freshwater might glimpse otters, beavers, and various fish species.

The unpredictability of wildlife encounters adds an element of excitement to RV camping. You never know when you might stumble upon a majestic elk grazing near your campsite or catch a glimpse of a colorful songbird perched on a branch. These unexpected moments create lasting memories and enhance the overall camping experience. It's not uncommon for campers to gather around a campfire in the evening and share stories of the day's wildlife sightings.

Wildlife photography is another popular pursuit during RV camping. Many RVers are avid photographers who bring their cameras and binoculars to capture stunning images of the natural world. Whether it's capturing the grace of a soaring bald eagle or the curiosity of a squirrel investigating a campsite, wildlife photography allows campers to preserve their memories and share their experiences with others.

While wildlife watching is a rewarding and enjoyable activity, it's important to practice responsible and ethical wildlife viewing. This includes respecting the animals' natural behaviors and habitats, maintaining a safe and respectful distance, and avoiding any actions that might disturb or harm them. Feeding wildlife or approaching them too closely can have negative consequences for both the animals and humans.

RV campers should also be mindful of the seasons and ecosystems they are exploring. Some wildlife species are more active and visible during specific times of the year or in particular habitats. By researching the local flora and fauna and understanding the seasonal patterns, campers can increase their chances of wildlife sightings.

Participating in organized wildlife tours and educational programs is another way to enhance the wildlife watching experience. Many national and state parks offer ranger-led programs and guided wildlife tours that provide valuable insights into the local ecosystems and the behaviors of the resident wildlife. These programs can be informative and entertaining, making them a great addition to an RV camping trip.

In conclusion, wildlife watching during RV camping is a delightful and enriching activity that allows campers to connect with the natural world and appreciate the beauty and diversity of wildlife. The convenience of RV camping in well-located campgrounds provides easy access to prime wildlife viewing areas, while the unpredictability of wildlife encounters adds an element of excitement and wonder to the experience. Whether it's observing birds, mammals, marine life, or insects, wildlife watching is a pastime that campers of all ages and skill levels can enjoy. As RVers immerse themselves in the natural surroundings of their campsites, they gain a deeper appreciation for the delicate balance of nature and the importance of preserving these habitats for future generations to enjoy.

Photography opportunities

RV camping offers a unique and rewarding opportunity for photography enthusiasts to capture the beauty of the great outdoors. Whether you're a seasoned photographer or just starting to explore the world of photography, the diverse landscapes, wildlife, and natural wonders encountered during RV camping trips provide a wealth of subjects and moments waiting to be captured through the lens of a camera.

One of the greatest advantages of photography during RV camping is the access it provides to a wide range of breathtaking landscapes. From majestic mountains and serene lakes to lush forests and picturesque coastlines, the scenery at campgrounds and RV parks can be truly inspiring. RVers can simply step outside their mobile homes and be greeted by stunning natural vistas, making capturing the perfect shot at any time of day convenient. The diversity of landscapes encountered during RV camping allows photographers to experiment with different photography styles and techniques. Wide-angle lenses can be used to capture sweeping landscapes, while telephoto lenses are ideal for wildlife and close-up shots. The changing lighting conditions throughout the day provide opportunities for capturing dynamic images, from the soft hues of sunrise and sunset to the harsh midday sun and the magic of golden hour.

Wildlife photography is another rewarding aspect of RV camping. Many campgrounds and RV parks are nestled in or near natural habitats where various wildlife species thrive. Birdwatchers can observe eagles soaring through the sky, songbirds perched on branches, or waterfowl gliding across the surface of a tranquil lake. Mammal enthusiasts may encounter deer, elk, bears, or other creatures, while coastal RV campers can capture shots of marine life such as dolphins, seals, and even whales.

The unpredictability of wildlife encounters adds an element of excitement and challenge to wildlife photography. Photographers must be patient, observant, and respectful of the animals' natural behaviors and habitats. The reward of capturing a stunning wildlife shot is a testament to one's photographic skills and the beauty and diversity of the natural world.

Furthermore, RV camping allows photographers to immerse themselves in the environments they wish to capture. Unlike day trips, camping provides the time and flexibility to thoroughly explore and photograph a location. Campers can revisit a favorite spot during different times of the day or week, allowing them to capture the landscape in various lighting conditions and moods. This depth of exploration often results in a more comprehensive and intimate photographic experience.

Night photography is yet another exciting aspect of RV camping. Away from the bright lights of cities, campgrounds and remote areas offer ideal conditions for astrophotography. Photographers can capture the majesty of the night sky, including the Milky Way, constellations, and meteor showers. Long exposure shots of campfires and starry skies can create mesmerizing images that convey the magic of nighttime in the wilderness.

While capturing stunning images is undoubtedly rewarding, it's also essential for photographers to focus on preserving and respecting the natural environment. The principles of Leave No Trace and ethical wildlife viewing should always be adhered to. This means leaving no trace of your presence, respecting wildlife habitats, and maintaining a safe and respectful distance from animals. Additionally, photographers should follow any rules and regulations established by the campground or park authorities to ensure the preservation of the area's natural beauty.

Numerous resources are available for those looking to enhance their photography skills during RV camping trips. Many campgrounds and national parks offer ranger-led photography programs and workshops. These educational opportunities provide valuable insights into photography techniques, equipment, and the unique challenges and opportunities the natural environment presents.

In conclusion, RV camping presents photography enthusiasts with an exceptional canvas to capture the beauty of the natural world. The convenience of RV living allows photographers to be immersed in diverse landscapes, while the unpredictability of wildlife encounters adds an element of excitement and challenge to their craft. RVers can experiment with various photography styles, from landscapes and wildlife to night photography. Moreover, camping provides the time and flexibility to explore and capture a location's essence thoroughly. As photographers seek to preserve the beauty of the great outdoors through their lenses, they also play a vital role in raising awareness about the importance of conservation and responsible outdoor recreation. RV camping and photography form a perfect synergy, offering a fulfilling and memorable experience for those who appreciate both photography's art and nature's wonders.

Water-based activities

One of the most alluring aspects of RV camping is the proximity to natural bodies of water, whether it be a serene lake, a meandering river, or the majestic ocean.

These aquatic environments offer many water-based activities that can significantly enhance the RV camping experience. Whether you're seeking relaxation or adventure, there's something for everyone to enjoy in the world of water-based activities while RV camping.

One of the simplest and most enjoyable water-based activities during RV camping is swimming. Many campgrounds and RV parks are located near swimming-friendly bodies of water, such as lakes or rivers. These natural swimming spots provide a refreshing escape from the summer heat and a great way to cool off after a day of outdoor activities. Additionally, some RV campgrounds offer swimming pools and water parks, providing a controlled and safe environment for families and individuals of all ages to enjoy.

Kayaking and canoeing are popular water activities that allow campers to explore the tranquil waters of lakes, rivers, and even coastal areas. These activities provide an intimate connection with nature, allowing campers to paddle at their own pace and explore secluded coves, wildlife-rich marshes, and picturesque shorelines. Many campgrounds offer kayak and canoe rentals, making it easy for RVers to access these watercraft and embark on their aquatic adventures.

Fishing is another cherished water-based activity during RV camping. Campers can cast their lines into nearby lakes, rivers, or ponds in search of various fish species. Fishing offers a sense of relaxation and serenity as anglers patiently wait for that exciting moment when a fish bites. Whether it's catch-and-release or keeping the day's catch for a campfire dinner, fishing adds an enjoyable dimension to the RV camping experience.

Boating is a versatile water activity ranging from leisurely cruises on a pontoon boat to thrilling adventures on speedboats or jet skis. Many RV campgrounds and lakeside locations offer boat rentals, allowing campers to explore the waterways and enjoy activities such as waterskiing, wakeboarding, or tubing. Boating also provides opportunities for picnics, birdwatching, and discovering hidden coves and islands.

For those passionate about aquatic wildlife, snorkeling and scuba diving offer the chance to explore the underwater world. RV camping near coastal areas or lakes with clear waters provides excellent opportunities for underwater exploration. Snorkeling allows campers to observe marine life, corals, and underwater landscapes with ease, while scuba diving offers a more immersive experience for certified divers to venture deeper into the depths of the water.

Stand-up paddleboarding (SUP) has gained popularity as a water-based activity that combines balance, fitness, and the opportunity to enjoy the water uniquely. Many campgrounds and lakeside locations offer SUP rentals, making it accessible for RV campers of all skill levels. Paddlers can cruise along the water's surface, enjoying the tranquility and breathtaking views while engaging in a full-body workout.

Camping near the ocean opens up a world of additional water-based activities, such as surfing, bodyboarding, and beachcombing. Surfers can catch waves, while bodyboarders can ride the shore break. The beachcombing experience allows campers to discover seashells, driftwood, and other treasures washed ashore by the tides. Oceanfront RV camping also provides an ideal setting for beach picnics, sandcastle building, and watching stunning sunsets over the water.

For RVers who enjoy a slower pace and a closer connection to nature, birdwatching and wildlife observation along water bodies are captivating activities. Lakes, rivers, and coastal areas often serve as habitats for various bird species, including waterfowl, eagles, herons, and shorebirds. Patient observation can reward campers with sightings of these magnificent creatures in their natural environments.

Water-based activities during RV camping offer a multitude of options to suit various interests and preferences. Whether it's the tranquility of swimming, the adventure of kayaking, the excitement of fishing, or the relaxation of a scenic boat ride, campers can find the perfect aquatic experience to complement their RV camping trip. Moreover, the natural beauty and serenity of water bodies provide a sense of peace and rejuvenation, making water-based activities an integral part of the RV camping experience for those seeking to connect with nature and enjoy the wonders of the water.

CHAPTER VIII

Navigating the Parks Responsibly

Leave No Trace principles for RVers

As outdoor enthusiasts, RVers are fortunate to have the opportunity to explore the beauty of nature while enjoying the comforts of home on the road. However, with this privilege comes a responsibility to minimize our environmental impact. Leave No Trace principles provide a valuable framework for RVers to follow, ensuring they leave the natural world as pristine and unspoiled as they found it. These principles are ethical and essential for preserving our natural spaces' integrity for future generations.

The first Leave No Trace principle is to plan ahead and prepare. RVers should research their destinations, campground regulations, and the specific Leave No Trace guidelines for the area they plan to visit. Proper planning includes having adequate supplies, understanding waste disposal options, and knowing the weather and terrain to ensure a safe and enjoyable trip.

The second principle is to travel and camp on durable surfaces. RVers should stay on designated roads and camp only in established campsites. This minimizes soil erosion, protects fragile vegetation, and maintains the landscape's natural beauty. Off-road driving or camping can cause lasting damage to ecosystems.

The third principle is to dispose of waste properly. RVers should always follow campground rules for waste disposal, including using designated dump stations for sewage and wastewater. Gray water, which includes water from sinks and showers, should also be disposed of in approved locations to prevent contamination of water sources. Proper disposal helps protect water quality and wildlife habitats.

The fourth principle is to leave what you find. This principle encourages RVers to avoid picking plants, disturbing wildlife, or removing natural features as souvenirs. Instead, enjoy the beauty of nature without altering it in any way. Leaving natural objects and features undisturbed allows others to enjoy them as well.

The fifth principle is to minimize campfire impact. While campfires are a cherished camping tradition, RVers should use a campfire only if it's allowed and keep it small. Using a camp stove for cooking is a more eco-friendly option, as campfires can scar the landscape, deplete wood resources, and contribute to air pollution. If a campfire is permitted, use established fire rings and burn only small sticks and twigs, leaving larger logs untouched.

The sixth principle is to respect wildlife. RVers should observe animals from a distance and avoid feeding them. Feeding wildlife can disrupt natural behaviors, lead to conflicts, and harm animals and humans. Keeping a respectful distance allows wildlife to thrive in their natural habitats undisturbed.

The seventh principle is to be considerate of other visitors. RVers should maintain quiet hours, follow campground rules, and be mindful of their impact on other campers. This includes keeping noise levels down, respecting privacy, and being courteous and friendly to fellow outdoor enthusiasts. A positive and considerate attitude enhances the overall camping experience for everyone.

The eighth and final principle is always to leave no trace of your visit. This principle encapsulates the essence of Leave No Trace ethics. RVers should pack out all trash, litter, and food scraps, leaving their campsite and the surrounding area cleaner than they found it. This includes picking up microtrash, such as bottle caps and cigarette butts, which can have a significant impact on the environment.

Incorporating Leave No Trace principles into RV camping helps protect the environment and ensures a more enjoyable and sustainable outdoor experience for all. Responsible RVers have the opportunity to set a positive example for others and contribute to the preservation of our natural treasures. By planning ahead, respecting natural ecosystems, and adopting a Leave No Trace mindset, RVers can continue to enjoy the beauty of nature while being responsible stewards of the environment.

Wildlife safety

One of the great joys of RV camping is connecting with nature and observing wildlife in their natural habitats. Whether you're parked in a serene forest, near a picturesque lake, or within the boundaries of a national park, encounters with wildlife can be a memorable and enriching part of the RV camping experience. However, it's essential for RVers to prioritize wildlife safety for their well-being, the welfare of the animals, and the preservation of natural ecosystems.

The first and most crucial rule of wildlife safety for RVers is to keep a safe distance from wild animals. While it can be tempting to approach or feed wildlife for a closer encounter or a photo opportunity, doing so can have serious consequences. Wild animals, even seemingly docile ones, can become unpredictable or aggressive when they feel threatened, cornered, or provoked. Approaching too closely can stress the animals, disrupt their natural behaviors, and even lead to dangerous situations for both humans and wildlife.

To ensure wildlife safety, RVers should follow the "rule of thumb" – maintain a distance of at least 100 yards (or 300 feet) from large mammals such as bears, moose, and elk. Smaller animals, such as deer or birds, may require a shorter distance, but it's essential to use good judgment and err on the side of caution. Always observe wildlife from a safe and respectful distance, using binoculars or a telephoto lens to get a closer look without intrusion.

It's important to remember that wildlife safety includes avoiding direct contact and safeguarding your food and belongings. RVers should store food securely in sealed containers or bear-proof storage lockers to prevent wildlife from being attracted to your campsite. Never leave food unattended, and clean up thoroughly after meals. Food odors and improperly stored trash can attract wildlife, leading to unwanted and potentially dangerous encounters.

When wildlife safety is a priority, knowing the specific animals that may inhabit the area you're camping in is essential. Different animals have different habits and behaviors, and understanding their characteristics can help you minimize the risk of unwanted interactions. For example, some animals are more active at dawn and dusk, so being vigilant during these times can help prevent encounters.

In regions known for bear activity, RVers should take additional precautions. Using bear-resistant containers for food storage is highly recommended. It's also wise to make noise when hiking or moving around, as bears are more likely to avoid humans if they are aware of their presence. Carrying bear spray and knowing how to use it properly can be a lifesaving tool in bear country.

In coastal areas, where marine wildlife such as seals, sea lions, and whales are common, RVers should maintain a respectful distance when observing these creatures from the shoreline or a boat. Harassing or approaching marine mammals can disrupt their behavior and even be illegal everywhere.

Birdwatching is a popular pastime for RVers, and it's essential to do so in a way that respects wildlife safety. When observing nesting birds, be careful not to disturb their nests or cause them to abandon their young. Keep a reasonable distance and use binoculars or spotting scopes to minimize intrusion. Avoid trampling on fragile nesting areas, especially in beach and marsh habitats.

Wildlife safety also extends to the protection of pets. RVers who travel with dogs should be aware of the potential risks wildlife encounters pose. Pets should always be leashed when in areas where wildlife may be present. Unsupervised pets can provoke or be injured by wild animals, so keeping them under control and preventing them from chasing or approaching wildlife is essential.

It's also important to be aware of local regulations and guidelines regarding wildlife safety. Many national parks and wildlife refuges have specific rules to protect wildlife and visitors. These rules may include requirements for keeping a safe distance from wildlife, leash laws for pets, and restrictions on feeding or approaching animals. Being informed and following these regulations is essential to ensure a positive and responsible RV camping experience.

In conclusion, wildlife encounters can be one of the most memorable aspects of RV camping, offering the opportunity to connect with the natural world and appreciate its beauty. However, prioritizing wildlife safety is crucial for the well-being of humans and animals and for preserving natural ecosystems. By keeping a safe distance, securing food and belongings, and respecting wildlife habitats and regulations, RVers can enjoy the wonder of wildlife while ensuring that these magnificent creatures remain wild and undisturbed. Responsible wildlife viewing and safety practices contribute to the overall enjoyment of RV camping and help protect the precious natural resources that make outdoor adventures so special.

Managing waste and environmental impact

RV camping offers a unique and enjoyable way to explore the great outdoors while enjoying the comforts of home on wheels. However, with the convenience of RVs comes the responsibility of managing waste and minimizing the environmental impact of our travels. RVers need to adopt sustainable practices to ensure that the natural beauty and pristine landscapes we enjoy remain unspoiled for generations to come.

One of the primary waste management concerns for RVers is wastewater disposal. RVs have two types of wastewater: gray water and black water. Gray water is the wastewater from sinks, showers, and appliances, while black water is the sewage from toilets. Proper disposal of both types of wastewater is essential for environmental and public health reasons.

Many campgrounds and RV parks provide dump stations where RVers can safely and responsibly dispose of their black water and gray water. These dump stations have sewer connections and facilities for rinsing and flushing tanks. It's crucial to follow campground rules and regulations regarding wastewater disposal and to use dump stations as directed. Dumping black or gray water on the ground or into natural water sources is illegal and harmful to the environment.

For RVers who prefer a more off-grid experience, portable wastewater holding tanks, also known as tote tanks, can be helpful. These tanks allow RVers to transport their wastewater to a dump station without moving their entire RV. Portable tanks come in various sizes and can make the process of waste disposal more convenient and environmentally responsible.

In addition to wastewater management, responsible solid waste disposal is essential for RVers. Campers should always dispose of trash in designated receptacles provided by campgrounds or public lands. Littering or leaving trash behind not only spoils the beauty of natural areas but also poses a threat to wildlife and can lead to environmental contamination.

To further minimize waste and reduce environmental impact, RVers can adopt eco-friendly practices. One of the most effective ways to do this is by reducing single-use plastics and opting for reusable alternatives. This includes using refillable water bottles, reusable shopping bags, and cloth towels instead of disposable paper products. Reducing the use of disposable plastic utensils, plates, and straws can also significantly reduce waste.

Energy consumption is another area where RVers can minimize their environmental impact. Many RVs have solar panels and energy-efficient appliances that help conserve power. RVers can maximize energy efficiency by using LED lighting, turning off appliances and lights when not in use, and monitoring energy consumption to avoid overloading electrical systems.

Water conservation is vital for RVers, especially when camping in areas with limited water availability. RVers can reduce water waste by taking shorter showers, using water-saving fixtures, and promptly fixing leaks. Collecting and using rainwater for activities such as rinsing dishes or watering plants is another eco-friendly practice.

Camping in Leave No Trace areas, where access to facilities may be limited, requires even more significant commitment to waste management and environmental impact reduction. RVers should bring along eco-friendly camping products, such as biodegradable soap and toilet paper, to minimize the environmental impact of their stay. Additionally, practicing Leave No Trace principles, such as packing out all waste, respecting wildlife and habitats, and leaving natural features untouched, is essential to protect delicate ecosystems.

Composting toilets can be an excellent choice for those seeking to take their environmental responsibility to the next level. Composting toilets convert human waste into compost, reducing the need for black water tanks and traditional sewage disposal. They are environmentally friendly and can be used in remote areas with unavailable sewage hookups.

Recycling is a fundamental aspect of waste management for RVers. Many campgrounds and RV parks have recycling bins, making it easy for campers to recycle materials such as glass, aluminum, plastic, and paper. RVers should sort and dispose of their recyclables properly to reduce landfill waste and conserve resources. In conclusion, managing waste and minimizing environmental impact is a vital responsibility for RVers who enjoy the beauty of the great outdoors. Proper wastewater disposal, solid waste management, and eco-friendly practices are essential for preserving the environment and ensuring that natural landscapes remain unspoiled. By adopting sustainable practices, reducing waste, and following Leave No Trace principles, RVers can enjoy the freedom of RV camping while also being responsible stewards of the environment. These practices benefit the planet and contribute to the enjoyment and sustainability of RV camping for generations to come.

Fire safety in the great outdoors

RV camping provides a wonderful opportunity to connect with nature and enjoy the beauty of the great outdoors.

Campfires have long been a cherished tradition in camping, offering warmth, ambiance, and a gathering place for friends and family. However, with the privilege of enjoying campfires comes the responsibility of fire safety. RVers need to be well-informed and practice fire safety to prevent wildfires, protect natural ecosystems, and ensure the safety of fellow campers.

One of the first and most critical aspects of fire safety for RVers is to be aware of local regulations and fire restrictions. Many campgrounds and outdoor areas have specific rules and guidelines regarding campfires. These rules often depend on the current fire danger levels and weather conditions. RVers should always check with campground authorities or park rangers to understand the current fire restrictions and adhere to them diligently. When campfires are permitted, choosing a safe location for the fire pit or ring is essential. Campfires should be set up in established fire rings or designated areas, ensuring the flames are contained and controlled. RVers should clear the area around the fire pit of any flammable materials, such as dry leaves, grass, and branches, and maintain a safe distance from trees, shrubs, and tents.

Starting and maintaining a campfire safely requires proper fire-building techniques. RVers should use only dry and seasoned firewood, as green or damp wood can produce excessive smoke and sparks. Building a small fire and gradually adding larger pieces of wood is recommended. Using fire starters, newspaper, or kindling to ignite the fire can help avoid the use of flammable liquids such as gasoline or lighter fluid, which can be dangerous.

Once a campfire is burning, it's essential to keep it under control. RVers should never leave a fire unattended, and they should have a source of water nearby, such as a bucket or hose, to extinguish the flames if necessary. Campers should also keep a shovel on hand for managing the fire and burying embers after use. If the wind is strong, it's advisable to postpone or extinguish the fire, as gusty winds can quickly spread flames and sparks.

Proper fire safety includes the responsible use of firewood and the avoidance of overloading the fire pit. RVers should avoid burning large logs that extend beyond the fire pit's edges, as this can lead to the scattering of embers and sparks. Burning trash, plastics, or treated wood should be strictly avoided, as these materials can release toxic fumes and harm the environment.

When it's time to extinguish a campfire, RVers should do so thoroughly. Using water or a fire extinguisher, campers should douse the flames until there are no remaining embers or smoldering ashes. Stirring the ashes and pouring water over them is essential to ensure complete extinguishment. The fire pit should then be cool to the touch before leaving the area.

One of the most critical aspects of fire safety outdoors is being prepared for emergencies. RVers should have a well-stocked first aid kit on hand and be knowledgeable about basic first aid procedures. Additionally, having a communication device, such as a satellite phone or a reliable two-way radio, can be a lifesaver in remote camping areas where cell phone reception may be limited.

Fire safety also includes being prepared for unexpected changes in weather conditions. RVers should be aware of weather forecasts and have a plan in case of sudden rain, strong winds, or other adverse conditions that could affect the campfire or pose a danger to campers. Adequate shelter, warm clothing, and a backup heat source, such as a propane heater, can be essential for staying safe in challenging weather.

In conclusion, fire safety is a fundamental aspect of responsible RV camping in the great outdoors. By being informed, following local regulations, and practicing safe fire-building techniques, RVers can enjoy the warmth and ambiance of a campfire while minimizing the risk of wildfires and protecting the environment. A well-prepared camper is also equipped to handle emergencies and adverse weather conditions, ensuring a safe and enjoyable outdoor experience for themselves and their fellow campers. Fire safety is not only a responsibility but also an essential skill for those who wish to fully appreciate the beauty and serenity of the natural world while RV camping.

CHAPTER IX

Exploring Nearby Attractions

Off-the-beaten-path destinations

One of the most significant advantages of RV camping is the flexibility to explore off-the-beaten-path destinations that may not be accessible by traditional means of travel. While popular tourist destinations have their charm, venturing off the main highways and into lesser-known areas can lead to some of the most memorable and enriching experiences. RVers willing to embrace the road less traveled can discover hidden gems, breathtaking landscapes, and unique cultural experiences that make their journeys extraordinary.

One such off-the-beaten-path destination for RVers is the North Cascades National Park in Washington State. Often overshadowed by its more famous neighbors, Mount Rainier and Olympic National Park, the North Cascades offer pristine wilderness, rugged mountain terrain, and numerous opportunities for outdoor adventures. RVers can explore the park's extensive network of hiking trails, go fishing in its clear alpine lakes, and marvel at the awe-inspiring vistas from overlooks along the North Cascades Highway. The park is a haven for wildlife enthusiasts and photographers, with a chance to spot bears, eagles, and other native species. Camping in one of the park's quieter campgrounds or boondocking in the surrounding national forest lands provides a tranquil escape from the crowds.

For those seeking a taste of the Wild West and rugged desert landscapes, the Owyhee Canyonlands in Oregon is an off-the-beaten-path destination that promises solitude and stunning scenery. This remote region in southeastern Oregon features deep canyons, red rock formations, and the wild and scenic Owyhee River. RVers can explore the area's winding dirt roads, visit historic sites like the Birch Creek Ranch, and hike along the rim of the canyons for breathtaking views. Camping in the Owyhee Canyonlands is a primitive experience, with dispersed camping and limited facilities, but it offers a unique opportunity to disconnect from the modern world and immerse oneself in the natural beauty of the desert.

Heading east to the heartland of the United States, RVers can discover the charm of the Driftless Area, a region in the upper Midwest that escaped the flattening effects of glaciation during the last Ice Age. Encompassing parts of Wisconsin, Minnesota, Iowa, and Illinois, the Driftless Area is characterized by rolling hills, deep river valleys, limestone bluffs, and picturesque farms. RVers can explore quaint towns like Decorah, Iowa, and Spring Green, Wisconsin, where cultural attractions, artisanal food, and local breweries await. Outdoor enthusiasts can enjoy hiking, biking, and paddling in the region's many parks and natural areas. The Driftless Area's unique geological features make it a hidden gem for those seeking a peaceful and scenic RV adventure.

For RVers looking to immerse themselves in the rich history and culture of the American Southwest, the Acoma Pueblo in New Mexico offers a captivating off-the-beaten-path experience. Known as "Sky City," Acoma Pueblo is one of North America's oldest continuously inhabited communities, with roots dating back over a thousand years. Perched atop a sandstone mesa, Acoma Pueblo is a living testament to Native American heritage and traditions. RVers can take guided pueblo tours, explore the ancient dwellings, and purchase handmade pottery and crafts from local artisans. Camping options in the area include RV parks and campgrounds, providing an opportunity to learn about the pueblo's history and culture while enjoying the stunning desert vistas.

Venturing into the northern reaches of the United States, RVers can uncover the natural wonders of the Upper Peninsula of Michigan. This less-traveled region is renowned for its pristine lakes, dense forests, and the majestic Pictured Rocks National Lakeshore along the shores of Lake Superior. RVers can hike along the lakeshore's rugged cliffs, kayak in the crystal-clear waters, and visit the area's charming small towns like Munising and Marquette. The Upper Peninsula also boasts numerous waterfalls, making it a paradise for waterfall enthusiasts. With various campgrounds and boondocking opportunities in the national forests, RVers can experience the serenity and beauty of the Upper Peninsula without the crowds found in more touristy destinations.

In the heart of the Southwest, RVers can embark on a journey to the Gila Wilderness in New Mexico, a hidden gem that offers a rugged and untouched natural landscape. As the nation's first designated wilderness area, the Gila Wilderness remains a pristine expanse of mountains, canyons, and rivers. RVers can hike the historic Gila Cliff Dwellings National Monument, soak in the natural hot springs, and traverse the Continental Divide Trail. The Gila Wilderness is a paradise for birdwatchers and wildlife enthusiasts, with opportunities to spot golden eagles, black bears, and elusive jaguars. Camping options range from established campgrounds to primitive sites along the Gila River, providing a remote and tranquil RV camping experience.

In conclusion, RVers who are willing to explore off-the-beaten-path destinations are rewarded with unique and unforgettable experiences. Whether it's the remote beauty of the North Cascades, the rugged desert landscapes of the Owyhee Canyonlands, the cultural richness of Acoma Pueblo, the natural wonders of Michigan's Upper Peninsula, or the pristine wilderness of the Gila, these lesser-known areas offer a chance to escape the crowds and immerse oneself in the natural and cultural treasures of America. Off-the-beaten-path destinations provide a sense of adventure, discovery, and a deeper connection to the diverse landscapes and heritage of the United States, making them ideal for RVers seeking a truly remarkable travel experience.

Local culture and history

One of the most rewarding aspects of RV travel is immersing oneself in the rich tapestry of local culture and history. As RVers crisscross the country, they can explore diverse communities, engage with local traditions, and discover the stories that have shaped a region. Whether it's savoring regional cuisine, visiting historical sites, or attending cultural festivals, RVers can enhance their travel experiences by embracing the local culture and history they encounter along the way.

Food is often a delicious gateway to understanding local culture. RVers can embark on culinary adventures by trying regional specialties and dishes that reflect the flavors and traditions of a particular area. Each region offers a distinct culinary identity from gumbo in Louisiana and clam chowder in New England to Tex-Mex cuisine in Texas and barbecue in the South. Sampling local fare at restaurants, food trucks, and farmers' markets allows RVers to connect with the community and savor the essence of a place through its cuisine.

History comes to life as RVers explore the countless historical sites and landmarks scattered throughout the country. Visiting museums, battlefields, and historic districts provides insights into the events, people, and movements that have shaped the nation's identity. For example, RVers can delve into the history of the American

Revolution by touring sites like Independence Hall in Philadelphia and the battlefields of Saratoga or Gettysburg. Exploring the historic districts of Charleston, South Carolina, or St. Augustine, Florida, offers a glimpse into the country's colonial past. Learning about the civil rights movement can be a powerful experience when visiting landmarks like the National Civil Rights Museum in Memphis or the Edmund Pettus Bridge in Selma, Alabama.

Cultural festivals and events are a vibrant way to engage with local communities and experience their traditions. RVers can plan their trips around festivals celebrating music, art, food, and heritage. For instance, attending the New Orleans Jazz & Heritage Festival offers a unique opportunity to soak in the city's music and cultural vibrancy. RVers can participate in Native American powwows, join in traditional dances at Native American reservations, or celebrate the rich traditions of Hispanic culture during Cinco de Mayo festivities in the Southwest. These events provide entertainment and foster a deeper understanding of the local culture and its significance to the community.

RVers seeking a more immersive cultural experience can engage with local artisans and craftsmen. Many communities have thriving arts scenes, with galleries, studios, and craft shops showcasing the work of talented artists. Whether it's pottery in New Mexico, handcrafted jewelry in the Southwest, or woodworking in the Appalachian Mountains, RVers can witness the creative process, meet artists, and acquire unique pieces that reflect the local culture and traditions.

Another way to connect with local culture and history is through storytelling and oral traditions. RVers can seek out local storytellers, historians, and tour guides who can offer insights into the area's past and present. Listening to the narratives of those who have lived in the region for generations can provide a deeper appreciation of the land and its significance to the people who call it home.

Exploring the architecture of a region is like reading a visual history book. RVers can wander through historic neighborhoods and admire the diverse architectural styles that define a place's character. From Victorian homes in San Francisco's Painted Ladies to colonial-era buildings in New England and adobe structures in the Southwest, the architecture tells the story of a region's evolution and the influences that have shaped it.

Local culture and history also come alive through music and dance. RVers can seek out live performances, whether it's listening to country music in Nashville, blues in the Mississippi Delta, or folk music in the Appalachian Mountains. Many communities host dance performances and cultural events that showcase the traditions of various ethnic groups. Participating in dance workshops or simply enjoying the rhythms of local music can be a fun and enriching way to connect with a region's cultural heritage.

For those interested in the heritage of Native American communities, RVers can explore reservations and cultural centers that offer insight into indigenous traditions, art, and history. Visiting tribal museums, participating in cultural events, and engaging with tribal members provides a unique opportunity to learn about the rich heritage of Native American cultures.

In conclusion, embracing local culture and history enhances the RV travel experience, allowing RVers to connect with the heart and soul of the places they visit. Whether it's savoring regional cuisine, exploring historical sites, attending cultural festivals, or engaging with local artisans, RVers have countless opportunities to delve into the tapestry of American culture and history. These experiences deepen one's understanding of the country and foster a sense of connection and appreciation for the diverse communities and traditions that make the United States a rich and vibrant tapestry of cultures and histories. RV travel becomes a journey of discovery, where every destination offers a chance to explore and celebrate the local culture and history that make each place unique.

Dining and shopping recommendations

One of the joys of RV travel is the opportunity to explore new regions and indulge in the local cuisine and shopping experiences unique to each destination. Whether you're parked in a coastal town, a bustling city, or a remote wilderness area, dining and shopping are essential elements of the RV journey. Here are some recommendations to enhance your dining and shopping experiences as an RVer.

When it comes to dining, one of the pleasures of RV travel is trying regional specialties and local flavors. Each part of the country has its culinary identity, and RVers can savor various dishes that showcase the area's cultural heritage. Whether it's indulging in seafood on the coast, sampling barbecue in the South, or enjoying farm-to-table cuisine in the heartland, local restaurants and eateries offer a window into the region's food traditions. To maximize your dining experiences, consider seeking out restaurants that emphasize farm-fresh ingredients and support local producers. Many regions have a vibrant food scene focusing on sustainability and locally sourced products. Exploring farmers' markets can also be a delightful way to connect with the community and discover fresh produce, artisanal cheeses, baked goods, and other local treats. RVers can stock up on seasonal fruits and vegetables, handmade jams, and unique food products that make for memorable meals at their campsite.

Additionally, don't forget to explore the food trucks and street vendors that often offer delicious and affordable options. Food trucks have become a culinary phenomenon in many cities and towns, serving up a diverse range of cuisines, from gourmet burgers to ethnic street food. These mobile eateries can be a convenient and fun way to experience local flavors on the go.

When dining out in your RV travels, be sure to ask locals for recommendations. Locals often know the best-kept culinary secrets and can direct you to hidden gems that may not be in tourist guidebooks. You can also take advantage of online review platforms and apps to discover highly-rated restaurants and read reviews from fellow travelers.

In addition to dining, shopping is another enjoyable aspect of RV travel. Many towns and cities along your route will have unique shops, boutiques, and markets offering a wide range of goods. Exploring these local stores can provide a glimpse into the culture and craftsmanship of the area.

Artisan shops are a treasure trove for finding handmade and locally crafted items. Whether it's pottery, jewelry, textiles, or woodworking, these shops showcase the talent and creativity of local artisans. Purchasing handmade souvenirs supports the local economy and allows you to take home one-of-a-kind mementos from your journey.

Antique stores and flea markets are also worth exploring, as they often hold hidden treasures and vintage items that can add character to your RV or serve as unique gifts. You never know what unique find you might stumble upon during your shopping adventures.

For those interested in discovering the history and culture of a region, consider visiting museums and cultural centers. These institutions often have gift shops that offer educational materials, books, and souvenirs related to the area's heritage. Purchasing items from these shops can help you delve deeper into the history and traditions of the places you visit.

When shopping for everyday necessities, RVers can take advantage of local grocery stores, farmers' markets, and specialty shops to stock up on fresh ingredients and regional products. Trying local snacks, beverages, and ingredients can add an extra layer of authenticity to your RV meals. Additionally, supporting local businesses contributes to the vitality of the communities you visit.

Consider patronizing local RV dealerships and outdoor stores when shopping for camping and RV supplies. These businesses often have a selection of RV accessories, camping gear, and equipment tailored to the needs of RV travelers. Building relationships with local RV dealers can also be helpful in case you need repairs or services while on the road.

Consider planning your visits during special events and festivals to make your dining and shopping experiences even more enjoyable. Many regions host food festivals, craft fairs, and cultural celebrations that showcase their unique offerings. Attending these events can be a great way to immerse yourself in the local culture and discover various culinary delights and artisanal products.

In conclusion, dining and shopping are integral parts of the RV travel experience, allowing you to savor the flavors and traditions of each destination. Exploring local cuisine, farmers' markets, artisan shops, and cultural centers enhances your journey by providing a deeper connection to the places you visit. Whether you're enjoying regional specialties at a local restaurant, purchasing handmade crafts from local artisans, or stocking up on fresh ingredients for your campsite meals, embracing the dining and shopping opportunities along your route adds richness and authenticity to your RV adventures. RV travel is not just about the destinations but also about the culinary and cultural discoveries that enrich your journey.

Side trips and day excursions

RVing represents the perfect blend of adventure and comfort for avid travelers who choose to explore the world on wheels. The open road beckons, and with it comes the allure of discovering new destinations, picturesque landscapes, and hidden gems. While the journey itself is often the primary focus for RVers, it's essential not to overlook the potential for side trips and day excursions. These short detours can provide a more profound and more diverse travel experience, offering a chance to explore the beauty and culture of the regions you pass through.

One of the significant advantages of RV travel is the freedom it offers. With your own home on wheels, you can pause your journey and explore fascinating places along the way. Side trips can vary from a few hours to a day or two, allowing you to immerse yourself in local attractions, history, and cuisine without the need for extensive planning or booking accommodations. Whether you're a history buff, a nature enthusiast, or a food lover, there are side trips tailored to your interests.

Nature lovers will find countless opportunities to connect with the outdoors. Many RV routes pass through national parks, forests, and scenic byways that are perfect for quick nature excursions. Imagine waking up in your RV amidst towering redwoods in California's Humboldt Redwoods State Park, or parking by a pristine lake in Colorado's Rocky Mountain National Park. These side trips offer a chance to hike, fish, birdwatch, or simply bask in the tranquility of nature.

For history enthusiasts, side trips can be a captivating journey into the past. From Civil War battlefields in

Virginia to ancient pueblo ruins in New Mexico, the United States is brimming with historical sites that invite exploration. While on the road, consider detouring to immerse yourself in the rich tapestry of American history, gaining insights into the events, people, and cultures that have shaped the nation.

Foodies and culture seekers will also find side trips to satisfy their cravings. Explore local markets, food festivals, and regional delicacies as you navigate different states and towns. Savor authentic barbecue in Texas, indulge in lobster rolls in Maine, or sample wine in the Napa Valley. Alongside culinary adventures, consider visiting museums, art galleries, and cultural landmarks to delve into each destination's unique character.

In addition to the diverse range of experiences, side trips can provide a much-needed break from the monotony of long drives. They allow you to stretch your legs, clear your mind, and reenergize, ensuring your RV journey is enjoyable and comfortable. RVers often discover unexpected treasures while venturing off the beaten path, creating lasting memories and enriching their travel experiences.

To make the most of side trips and day excursions, it's advisable to plan ahead to some extent. Research potential stops along your route, check operating hours, and consider any necessary permits or reservations. Flexibility remains key, as spontaneity can lead to some of the most memorable discoveries.

In conclusion, side trips and day excursions are integral to the RVing experience, offering travelers the chance to explore the diversity of the American landscape, history, and culture. These detours provide opportunities for nature enthusiasts, history buffs, food lovers, and adventurers alike to create unforgettable moments along their journey. As you embark on your RV adventure, remember that it's not just about reaching your destination but also about embracing the enriching experiences that can be found along the way.

CHAPTER X

Staying Healthy and Safe

Health and medical considerations

For many people, living in an RV allows them to travel and explore while still having all the conveniences of home on wheels. It's essential for people who choose to travel nomadic to consider the particular health and medical difficulties that come with living on the road. Whether you're an occasional traveler or a full-time RVer, being aware of these factors and making plans for them will help to guarantee a fun and safe experience.

RVers should put routine medical exams and vaccinations first and foremost. When traveling, you might not always have easy access to medical facilities and might end up in isolated locations without quick access to care. The first line of defense against unanticipated medical issues is maintaining good health. Make sure your routine vaccinations are up to date, and make appointments for regular checkups to take care of any underlying health issues.

Insurance is a crucial component of living in an RV. Ensure you have sufficient health insurance that covers you in your home state as well as the places you intend to visit. Many RVers choose health insurance policies that provide coverage across the country or look into telemedicine options, which can be a great way to get medical advice and consultations while traveling.

For RVers, medications are essential, particularly if you have long-term medical issues. Always keep a copy of your prescriptions with you and a sufficient supply of your prescribed medications. If you need medical attention while traveling or refilling prescriptions, it's a good idea to research the pharmacies and hospitals in the areas you intend to visit.

Maintaining a healthy lifestyle is the secret to general wellbeing when living in an RV. Maintaining healthy eating habits, drinking plenty of water, and exercising frequently are essential while traveling. With the ease of meal preparation provided by RV kitchens, you can better manage your diet. Including physical activity in your daily routine can also help you stay in shape and energized. Examples of this include hiking in national parks and doing yoga at your campsite.

Sleep quality should not be underestimated while RVing. Physical and mental well-being depend on getting a good night's sleep, and getting used to new sleeping arrangements can be difficult. Invest in a cozy mattress and blackout curtains in your RV, and create a nighttime routine that encourages sound sleep.

RVers need to take extra safety measures because accidents can occur. Ensure your first aid kit is fully stocked and you know about the fundamentals of first aid. Learning how to use an automated external defibrillator (AED) and performing CPR in an emergency are also wise moves. Think about signing up for a roadside assistance program that provides services related to vehicles as well as medical assistance.

The mental well-being of RVers is frequently disregarded. With the requirement to adjust to new surroundings and occasionally cope with isolation, the lifestyle can be both rewarding and challenging. Keeping in touch with family and friends through social media, video chats, or phone calls can help fight feelings of isolation. Find encouraging RV communities and partake in joyful and fulfilling activities as well.

In conclusion, health and medical concerns are essential for RVers to have a happy and safe travel experience. Essential actions include carrying necessary prescriptions and first aid supplies, maintaining adequate insurance coverage, and prioritizing routine health checkups. Other crucial aspects include adopting a healthy lifestyle, making sure you get enough sleep, and taking precautions. Finally, remember the value of maintaining relationships with family, friends, supportive communities, and your mental health. RVers can confidently travel knowing they are ready for anything that may arise while traveling by taking these factors into account before setting out on their journey.

Emergency preparedness

The nomadic lifestyle of RVing is an enticing adventure, allowing travelers to explore the world's beauty from the comfort of their mobile homes. While the open road may promise freedom and excitement, RVers need to prioritize emergency preparedness. Being well-prepared for unforeseen circumstances can distinguish between a minor inconvenience and a potentially life-threatening situation. This section will explore the critical aspects of emergency preparedness for RVers to ensure their safety and peace of mind on the road.

First and foremost, RVers should have a comprehensive emergency plan in place. This plan should include a clear communication strategy, contact information for emergency services, and designated meeting points for family or travel companions. Ensure everyone on board is familiar with the plan and knows what to do in an emergency.

One of the most critical aspects of emergency preparedness is having a well-equipped first aid kit readily available. Your first aid kit should include essential medical supplies, such as bandages, antiseptic wipes, pain relievers, adhesive tape, and scissors. Additionally, consider adding specific items tailored to your needs, such as prescription medications, EpiPens, or personal medical devices.

For RVers, reliable communication is essential during emergencies. Ensure you have a working cell phone with a charged battery and access to a mobile network or satellite phone, especially if you plan to travel to remote areas with limited cell coverage. Emergency radio devices, like a NOAA weather radio, can also provide critical weather alerts and updates.

Another crucial aspect of preparedness is having a sufficient supply of essential resources. This includes food, water, and fuel. Stock your RV with non-perishable food items, enough drinking water for all passengers, and extra fuel for your generator or vehicle. Remember that access to grocery stores or gas stations may be limited or temporarily unavailable during particular emergencies.

RVers should also be equipped to handle extreme weather conditions. Depending on your travel destination and the time of year, you may encounter inclement weather like storms, heavy rain, or extreme heat. Wear appropriate clothing, blankets, and gear to stay warm or cool. Invest in weather-appropriate tires, tire chains, and equipment to navigate through challenging road conditions.

Fire safety is a top priority for RVers, given the close quarters of a motorhome or trailer. Install and regularly test smoke detectors and carbon monoxide alarms in your RV. Equip your RV with fire extinguishers and know how to use them. Establish fire safety protocols and escape routes, especially if you're traveling with family or pets. Additionally, it's wise to familiarize yourself with your destination's emergency services and resources. Research nearby hospitals, clinics, and emergency rooms, and have a list of their addresses and contact information on hand. Understanding the local emergency response procedures and the nearest evacuation routes can be crucial in times of crisis.

Lastly, consider joining a roadside assistance program that offers emergency services for RVers. These programs can provide towing, vehicle repair, and even temporary accommodations if your RV becomes inoperable due to an accident or mechanical failure.

In conclusion, emergency preparedness is a fundamental aspect of RVing that cannot be overlooked. A well-thought-out emergency plan, a fully stocked first aid kit, reliable communication, and access to essential resources are all vital components of ensuring your safety while on the road. Understanding how to handle extreme weather conditions, prioritizing fire safety, and researching local emergency services at your destination are also essential. By taking these precautions, RVers can confidently embark on their adventures, knowing they are well-prepared to handle any unexpected challenges that may arise during their travels.

Personal safety on the road

The RV lifestyle is an enticing and liberating way to explore the world, allowing travelers to roam freely while carrying the comforts of home on wheels. However, like any form of travel, personal safety should remain a top priority for RVers. Whether you're a full-time RVer or embarking on a temporary adventure, there are essential measures to ensure your well-being while on the road.

First and foremost, RVers should prioritize situational awareness. Being aware of your surroundings and paying attention to your intuition can go a long way in avoiding potentially unsafe situations. When parking at a campsite or rest area, assess the area for signs of security, such as good lighting and the presence of other campers. Trust your instincts; if something feels off, consider relocating to a more secure location.

It's also crucial to secure your RV properly. Lock all doors and windows when leaving your vehicle unattended, even temporarily. Invest in quality locks and security systems to deter potential intruders. When camping in remote areas, consider using motion-activated outdoor lighting to illuminate the surroundings and deter wildlife or unwanted visitors.

Another significant aspect of personal safety on the road is communication. Make sure you have a reliable means of communication, such as a cell phone or satellite phone, with a charged battery and access to a mobile network. Share your travel plans with a trusted friend or family member, including your intended route, destinations, and expected arrival times. Having someone aware of your itinerary can be invaluable in case of emergencies. Traveling with a companion can enhance personal safety. In addition to the companionship, having an extra pair of eyes and ears can provide an added layer of security. You can watch out for each other, share responsibilities, and provide assistance if needed.

When it comes to personal belongings, exercise caution and discretion. Avoid displaying expensive items, such as electronics or jewelry, in plain sight, as this can attract unwanted attention. Consider using safes or hidden compartments within your RV to secure valuable possessions when you're away from your vehicle. Planning and research are essential for personal safety as well. Before embarking on a trip, familiarize yourself with the areas you'll be visiting. Research the local crime rates, common safety concerns, and any travel advisories. This information can help you decide where to stay and when to be more cautious.

Trustworthy RV communities can also provide an additional layer of safety. Engage with fellow RVers, participate in group activities, and join online forums or social media groups for RV enthusiasts. These connections can offer valuable advice, support, and a sense of security when you're on the road.

Lastly, consider personal safety items, such as pepper spray or personal alarms, for added protection. While it's essential to hope for the best, being prepared for unexpected situations can make all the difference in personal safety.

In conclusion, personal safety is paramount for RVers as they embark on their journeys. Critical measures include prioritizing situational awareness, securing your RV, and maintaining effective communication. Traveling with a companion, exercising discretion with personal belongings, and conducting thorough research on destinations can further enhance safety. Engaging with RV communities and considering personal safety items are additional precautions to ensure a safe and enjoyable RV adventure. By taking these measures, RVers can confidently explore the world, knowing they are well-equipped to protect their safety while on the road.

Coping with unexpected challenges

The allure of the open road, the freedom to explore new places, and the comforts of home on wheels make RVing an appealing lifestyle for many. However, the reality of life on the road is not always as idyllic as it may seem. RVers, whether full-time or occasional travelers, often encounter unexpected challenges that can test their adaptability and resilience. In this section, we will explore how RVers can cope with these unforeseen hurdles and continue to enjoy their nomadic adventures.

One of the most common unexpected challenges RVers face is mechanical breakdowns or vehicle-related issues. Whether it's a flat tire, engine trouble, or a malfunctioning appliance, these situations can disrupt travel plans and create stress. To cope with such challenges, it's crucial to be prepared. Regular maintenance and vehicle inspections can help identify potential problems before they escalate. Additionally, having a basic knowledge of RV repairs and carrying essential tools can be invaluable. Joining a roadside assistance program can provide peace of mind, knowing that help is just a phone call away in case of a breakdown.

Weather-related challenges are another aspect of RV life that can catch travelers off guard. Sudden storms, extreme temperatures, and adverse road conditions can impact both safety and comfort. RVers should stay informed about the weather forecast and plan their routes accordingly. Investing in quality tires suitable for various weather conditions and carrying necessary equipment like tire chains can help navigate challenging road conditions. Proper insulation, ventilation, and climate control within the RV can ensure a comfortable interior regardless of the weather outside.

Navigational challenges can also arise, especially when exploring remote or unfamiliar areas. GPS devices and navigation apps are valuable but not infallible tools. RVers should have backup navigation methods, such as paper maps and compasses, to cope with unexpected detours, road closures, or inaccurate directions. Staying open to alternate routes and embracing the unexpected can lead to serendipitous discoveries and memorable adventures. Health-related challenges, such as illnesses or injuries, can be particularly unsettling for RVers, as access to medical care may be limited in remote areas. To cope with these challenges, carrying a well-stocked first aid kit and being knowledgeable about basic first aid procedures is essential. Additionally, maintaining good health through proper nutrition, regular exercise, and adequate rest can help prevent health issues from arising in the first place. Having reliable health insurance and knowing the locations of nearby medical facilities are also crucial considerations.

Safety concerns, including theft, accidents, or encounters with wildlife, are part of the RVing experience. Coping with these challenges requires vigilance and precaution. Secure your RV when you're away, be mindful of your surroundings, and follow safety guidelines for wildlife encounters. Engaging with fellow RVers and staying informed about safety tips for specific areas can provide valuable insights and added protection.

Lastly, adapting to unexpected challenges often comes down to having a positive attitude and a flexible mindset. RVing is about embracing the unknown and learning from each experience, whether it's a challenging situation or a delightful surprise. Finding humor in adversity and sharing stories with fellow travelers can foster a sense of camaraderie and resilience.

In conclusion, RVers must be prepared to face unexpected challenges as they navigate the open road. Coping with vehicle issues, adverse weather conditions, navigational hiccups, health concerns, and safety considerations requires a combination of preparedness, knowledge, and adaptability. By being proactive and maintaining a positive outlook, RVers can transform unexpected challenges into opportunities for personal growth and memorable adventures.

CHAPTER XI

Wrapping Up Your Adventure

Packing up and preparing to leave

The thrill of RV camping is undeniable. Exploring picturesque landscapes, connecting with nature, and enjoying the freedom of the open road are all part of the adventure. However, as your camping trip comes to an end, the process of packing up and preparing to leave can be a bit daunting. It's essential to approach this phase with organization and care to ensure a smooth departure and to leave the campsite as you found it.

First and foremost, start by creating a checklist. Having a comprehensive list of items to pack and tasks to complete can help you stay organized and ensure that nothing is forgotten. The checklist should include everything from personal belongings to camping gear, kitchen supplies, and waste disposal necessities.

Begin by cleaning and tidying up your campsite. Collect all trash, food scraps, and debris, and dispose of them properly in designated receptacles. Leave-no-trace principles should guide all campers, ensuring that you leave the natural environment as pristine as you found it. Scrub and clean your campsite area, including the grill, picnic table, and cooking equipment.

Once the campsite is clean, focus on your RV's interior. Start by securing all loose items to prevent them from shifting during travel. Close and lock all windows and doors. Empty and clean your refrigerator, ensuring no perishable items are left behind. Secure appliances, cabinets, and drawers to prevent them from opening while driving. Don't forget to double-check that all electrical appliances and systems are turned off.

Before departing, it's crucial to handle waste disposal properly. Empty your RV's holding tanks at the designated dump station, ensuring that you follow campground rules and guidelines. Clean and sanitize the tanks as needed to prevent odors and buildup.

Next, prepare your RV's exterior for departure. Retract and secure any awnings, slide-outs, or stabilizers that were deployed during your stay. Check tire pressure and inspect the tires for any signs of damage or wear. Ensure all hitching and towing equipment is connected correctly and locked in place.

As you prepare to leave, taking safety precautions is essential. Double-check that your RV's brake lights, turn signals, and headlights function correctly. Test the brakes and make sure they are in good working order. Familiarize yourself with your RV's weight distribution and handling characteristics to ensure safe driving.

Before leaving your campsite, take a final walk around to ensure nothing has been left behind. It's easy to overlook small items like camping chairs, trash bags, or personal items, so a thorough inspection is essential.

When you're ready to hit the road, be mindful of your departure time. It's courteous to leave reasonably, respecting the campground's quiet hours and check-out policies. Bid farewell to fellow campers and thank campground staff for a pleasant stay.

During your drive, be cautious and attentive, especially if you're traveling on winding or unfamiliar roads. Keep an eye on traffic signs, follow speed limits, and be prepared for sudden changes in weather or road conditions. It's also wise to have a plan for your next destination, including campground reservations if needed, to avoid any last-minute uncertainties.

In conclusion, packing up and preparing to leave after RV camping is crucial to the overall camping experience. You can ensure a smooth and efficient departure by following an organized checklist, cleaning and tidying your campsite, handling waste disposal responsibly, and ensuring safety precautions. Leaving your campsite in pristine condition respects the environment and sets a positive example for fellow campers and future visitors. Ultimately, the combination of careful preparation and responsible camping practices allows RV enthusiasts to enjoy the beauty of the outdoors while leaving minimal impact behind.

Reflections on your RV journey

As your RV journey ends, whether it's a weekend getaway or an extended expedition, it's a natural time to reflect on the experiences, memories, and lessons learned along the way. RVing is not just a mode of travel; it's a lifestyle that offers a unique perspective on the world and a chance to connect with nature, people, and oneself. Here, we delve into some of the key reflections that often emerge at the conclusion of an RV journey.

First and foremost, RVing provides a renewed appreciation for the beauty of the natural world. From national parks to remote wilderness areas, the journey takes you to some of the most stunning landscapes on Earth. The awe-inspiring vistas, diverse ecosystems, and breathtaking sunsets are constant reminders of the planet's natural wonders. RVers often find themselves reconnecting with nature profoundly, fostering a deep sense of gratitude for the environment and a commitment to its preservation.

Another reflection that arises from an RV journey is realizing the importance of simplicity and minimalism. Living in a confined space necessitates prioritizing essential items and shedding the unnecessary. This simplification process can be liberating, freeing you from the burden of material possessions and reminding you that happiness can be found in experiences rather than possessions.

Community and human connections play a significant role in the RV lifestyle. RVers often form close-knit bonds with fellow travelers they meet on the road. Campfires, potluck dinners, and shared stories at campgrounds create a sense of camaraderie that transcends geographical boundaries. These connections remind us of the commonality of human experiences and the beauty of diverse perspectives.

Self-discovery is another reflection that often emerges during an RV journey. The solitude and introspection that come with traveling in an RV allow for a deeper exploration of one's thoughts, desires, and values. Many RVers find themselves reconnecting with their passions, discovering new interests, or gaining clarity about their life goals.

The RV journey also teaches adaptability and resilience. Navigating unfamiliar roads, handling unexpected challenges, and embracing change become part of the daily routine. These experiences cultivate a sense of flexibility and the ability to thrive in ever-changing circumstances.

One of the most potent reflections that RVers often express is the appreciation for the present moment. Life on the road encourages mindfulness, as you savor each sunset, cherish each conversation, and immerse yourself in the sights and sounds of your surroundings. The constant change and the knowledge that moments are fleeting reinforce the importance of living in the here and now.

The RV journey is not without its challenges and inconveniences, but precisely these moments lead to growth and self-improvement. Overcoming obstacles, learning new skills, and pushing the boundaries of comfort zones are part of the RV experience. These challenges become opportunities for personal development and resilience-building.

In conclusion, an RV journey is not just a physical adventure; it's a transformative and reflective journey of the mind and spirit. It offers a chance to reconnect with nature, simplify life, forge meaningful connections, and discover oneself in new ways. It encourages adaptability and mindfulness and reminds us of the importance of living fully in the present moment. As you conclude your RV journey, take the time to reflect on the profound impact it has had on your life and the enduring lessons that will continue to shape your perspective long after the road trip ends.

Documenting your travels

Embarking on an RV journey is a thrilling adventure filled with breathtaking scenery, unique experiences, and unforgettable moments. Whether exploring the wonders of the national parks, visiting charming small towns, or taking the road less traveled, documenting your RV travels can enhance your experience and create lasting memories. In this section, we explore the various ways to document your RV journeys and why it's a rewarding practice for RV enthusiasts.

One of the most popular ways to document your RV travels is through photography. Capturing stunning landscapes, cozy campfires, and candid moments with fellow travelers allows you to relive the beauty and excitement of your journey long after it's over. You don't need a high-end camera to get started; a smartphone with a good camera can be a powerful tool for capturing memories. Organize your photos by date or location, and consider creating a dedicated album or digital gallery to keep your travel memories organized.

Another creative way to document your RV travels is by keeping a travel journal or blog. Writing down your thoughts, experiences, and reflections can be a deeply rewarding practice. A travel journal allows you to document the places you've visited and the emotions and personal insights you've gained along the way. If you prefer digital platforms, starting a travel blog or using social media to share your journey with friends and fellow travelers can be an engaging way to connect and inspire others.

Vlogging, or creating video content, is becoming increasingly popular among RVers. With today's technology, it's easier than ever to document your travels through video. You can capture stunning drone footage, record interviews with locals, or simply share your day-to-day experiences. Video allows you to convey the sights, sounds, and emotions of your journey dynamically. Platforms like YouTube allow reaching a broader audience and connecting with fellow RV enthusiasts.

Scrapbooking is a traditional but artistic way to document your RV travels. Collecting postcards, brochures, maps, and mementos from your journey and arranging them in a scrapbook can create a tangible and visually appealing record of your adventures. Add personal notes, captions, and artwork to make your scrapbook a unique and cherished keepsake.

Travel apps and digital tools can streamline the process of documenting your RV travels. There are apps designed specifically for tracking your route, recording expenses, and finding campgrounds or points of interest along the way. Utilizing these tools can help you stay organized and easily retrieve important information about your journey.

Documenting your RV travels is not just about creating a record of where you've been; it's also about preserving the stories and emotions associated with those places. These documented memories become valuable for planning future trips, sharing your adventures with loved ones, and reflecting on your personal growth and experiences. It allows you to relive the joy of your RV journey long after you've returned home.

In conclusion, documenting your RV travels is a rewarding and creative practice that enhances your overall travel experience. Whether through photography, journaling, vlogging, scrapbooking, or digital tools, finding a method that resonates with you can help preserve the beauty and significance of your adventures. Documenting your travels creates lasting memories and allows you to connect with others, share your passion for RVing, and inspire fellow travelers to embark on their own unforgettable journeys.

Planning for future adventures

For RV enthusiasts, the end of one journey marks the beginning of the next. The RV lifestyle offers endless opportunities for exploration, and as you conclude one adventure, it's natural to start planning for future RV journeys. Whether you dream of visiting iconic national parks, discovering hidden gems, or embarking on extended road trips, thoughtful planning is key to turning your RV dreams into reality. This section will explore the importance of planning for future RV adventures and provide some valuable tips to help you get started.

The first step in planning for future RV adventures is setting clear goals and defining your travel priorities. Ask yourself what type of experiences you want, whether exploring new landscapes, immersing yourself in local cultures, or enjoying outdoor activities like hiking or fishing. Knowing your preferences will guide your travel plans and help you select destinations and routes that align with your interests.

Research is an essential part of the planning process. Begin by exploring potential travel destinations and creating a list of places you want to visit. Utilize travel guides, websites, and online forums to gather information about campgrounds, attractions, and local events. Consider climate, seasonal variations, and travel restrictions when determining the best time to visit specific destinations.

Budgeting for your RV adventures is a critical aspect of planning. RV travel costs can vary significantly based on fuel, campground fees, dining expenses, and entertainment. Create a detailed budget that accounts for all potential costs, including maintenance and repairs for your RV. A clear understanding of your financial requirements will help you plan and save accordingly.

When planning for future RV adventures, it's essential to establish a rough itinerary. While leaving room for spontaneity and flexibility is part of the RV charm, having a primary route and schedule in mind can provide structure and ensure that you don't miss out on must-see destinations. Be realistic about the distances you can comfortably cover in a day and allocate time for rest and relaxation.

Making campground reservations in advance is crucial, especially during peak travel seasons. Popular campgrounds can fill up quickly, so booking your spots as early as possible is advisable to secure your preferred accommodations. Some campgrounds even offer discounts for reservations made well in advance.

Safety should always be a priority when planning RV adventures. Ensure your RV is in good working condition by scheduling regular maintenance checks and promptly addressing necessary repairs. Invest in safety equipment such as tire pressure monitors, smoke detectors, and carbon monoxide alarms. Familiarize yourself with the emergency procedures for your RV and create a well-stocked emergency kit.

As you plan for future RV adventures, don't forget to review and update your insurance coverage. Ensure your RV insurance policy provides adequate coverage for your planned travels, including liability, comprehensive, and collision coverage. Consider adding personal belongings and roadside assistance coverage to provide additional peace of mind.

Lastly, embrace the sense of anticipation and excitement that comes with planning for future RV adventures. Share your travel plans with friends and fellow RV enthusiasts, gather travel tips and recommendations, and create a task checklist before hitting the road. The planning process itself can be a joyful part of the RV experience, filled with anticipation and the promise of new adventures.

In conclusion, planning for future RV adventures is an essential and rewarding part of the RV lifestyle. Setting clear goals, conducting research, budgeting, creating an itinerary, making reservations, ensuring safety, and reviewing insurance coverage are all crucial steps in planning. Embrace the excitement of looking ahead to new journeys, and let the anticipation of future RV adventures inspire and motivate you to explore the world in your home on wheels.

CONCLUSION

In conclusion, "Recreational Wonders: Navigating National Parks in Your Home on Wheels" has been a comprehensive guide to the thrilling world of RV travel within America's breathtaking national parks. We've embarked on a journey from the initial dream of hitting the open road to the practicalities of choosing the right RV, planning your route, and experiencing the diverse beauty of our national treasures.

Throughout this book, we've explored the allure of the RV lifestyle, the essential equipment and accessories, budgeting considerations, and the seasonal nuances that shape your RV travel experience. We've discussed the importance of reservations and permits, allowing you to navigate the intricacies of securing your spot within these pristine natural landscapes.

As we conclude this RV travel adventure, we hope you're equipped with the knowledge, confidence, and inspiration needed to embark on your unforgettable journey. The call of the wild, the allure of the open road, and the enchantment of America's national parks are waiting for you to explore.

Remember, RV travel is not just a mode of transportation; it's a lifestyle that offers freedom, adventure, and the chance to connect with the majesty of nature. Whether you're a solo traveler, a couple seeking romance on the road, or a family creating lasting memories together, the RV lifestyle promises awe-inspiring experiences and the thrill of discovery.

So, fasten your seatbelt, rev up the engine of your home on wheels, and let the wonder of RV travel guide you to some of the most incredible and captivating places our nation has to offer. Your journey starts now, and the recreational wonders of America's national parks await your exploration. Safe travels, fellow adventurers, and may your RV journey be filled with beauty, serenity, and a sense of wonder that knows no bounds.

www.ingramcontent.com/pod-product-compliance
Lightning Source LLC
Chambersburg PA
CBHW052044150726

48002CB00002B/745